Beginning ChatGPT for Python

Build Intelligent Applications with OpenAI APIs

Lydia Evelyn
Bruce Hopkins

Apress®

Beginning ChatGPT for Python: Build Intelligent Applications with OpenAI APIs

Lydia Evelyn
Catalonia, Huesca, Spain

Bruce Hopkins
Orlando, FL, USA

ISBN-13 (pbk): 979-8-8688-0928-6
https://doi.org/10.1007/979-8-8688-0929-3

ISBN-13 (electronic): 979-8-8688-0929-3

Managing Director, Apress Media LLC: Welmoed Spahr
Acquisitions Editor: Celestin Suresh John
Development Editor: James Markham
Coordinating Editor: Gryffin Winkler

Cover designed by eStudioCalamar

Distributed to the book trade worldwide by Apress Media, LLC, 1 New York Plaza, New York, NY 10004, U.S.A. Phone 1-800-SPRINGER, fax (201) 348-4505, e-mail orders-ny@springer-sbm.com, or visit www.springeronline.com. Apress Media, LLC is a California LLC and the sole member (owner) is Springer Science + Business Media Finance Inc (SSBM Finance Inc). SSBM Finance Inc is a **Delaware** corporation.

For information on translations, please e-mail booktranslations@springernature.com; for reprint, paperback, or audio rights, please e-mail bookpermissions@springernature.com.

Apress titles may be purchased in bulk for academic, corporate, or promotional use. eBook versions and licenses are also available for most titles. For more information, reference our Print and eBook Bulk Sales web page at http://www.apress.com/bulk-sales.

Any source code or other supplementary material referenced by the author in this book is available to readers on GitHub (https://github.com/Apress). For more detailed information, please visit https://www.apress.com/gp/services/source-code.

If disposing of this product, please recycle the paper

Table of Contents

About the Authors

Lydia Evelyn is a proficient technical writer and a skilled Python developer with a professional background in ChatGPT. She has effectively utilized ChatGPT, coupled with prompt engineering, in multiple client projects within the realm of technical publishing. Lydia boasts extensive programming expertise in both Python and Java.

Bruce Hopkins is an accomplished author and technical writer. Bruce's focus has been on pioneering research in natural language processing (NLP) and artificial intelligence (AI), particularly in the domain of speech and chatbot applications. He holds the distinguished title of an Intel Innovator for AI and IoT.

About the Technical Reviewer

 **Sergei Sinenkov** is a software developer. He holds a Master's degree in International Commerce and Finance from the University of Barcelona, Faculty of Economics and Business. Additionally, he completed a Bachelor's degree in Mathematical Methods in Economics at N.I. Lobachevsky State University of Nizhny Novgorod, within the Faculty of Mechanics and Mathematics.

Working as a software developer since 2008, he has a lot of experience in back-end development and in the database area. Throughout his career, he has developed a variety of systems using Python and other programming languages, integrating them with databases and enterprise software systems.

CHAPTER 1

Introducing ChatGPT for Python Developers

Who Is This Book For?

First of all, this book is for Python developers who don't have any training or experience in artificial intelligence, natural language processing, machine learning, or deep learning. You may have heard of the term "language model," but I'm going to assume that it's *not* a term that you use every day.

Secondarily, you might be familiar with (or have tried) ChatGPT, but you don't *quite* understand how everything works "under the hood," and you're not sure how to get started in order to use Python and ChatGPT programmatically together to "AI enable" your own applications and services.

Note   Although ChatGPT is a household name, OpenAI, the company behind it, lacks broad recognition and isn't as widely recognized. So, although this book is about how to use ChatGPT programmatically within your Python apps, the APIs that we will be using are officially the OpenAI REST APIs. Therefore, we'll be using the term "ChatGPT API" and "OpenAI API" synonymously.

© Lydia Evelyn, Bruce Hopkins 2024
L. Evelyn and B. Hopkins, *Beginning ChatGPT for Python*, https://doi.org/10.1007/979-8-8688-0929-3_1

Overview

In this chapter, we're going to dive right in and explain a few terms that you might not be familiar with, and then go straight to the ChatGPT Playground. The Playground is essentially a web interface for developers that's built on top of ChatGPT REST API. So, once you're familiar with the Playground, the calls and responses from the ChatGPT API will feel like second nature to you.

Download the Code Now!

This book is filled with tons of examples and example code, so why bother typing everything yourself? Below is the URL to the GitHub repo to access the source code:

https://github.com/Apress/Beginning-ChatGPT-for-Python

So, What Exactly Is ChatGPT and Why Do I Need to Use the OpenAI APIs?

Simply stated, ChatGPT is a group of **language models** (which are the result of training deep learning algorithms) developed by OpenAI that is capable of generating humanlike text responses based on given prompts. So, what's a prompt? A prompt is simply the input text that you give to ChatGPT. So, let's kick things off by giving ChatGPT a prompt to ask how well it's familiar with Python design patterns.

Listing 1-1. PROMPT. A Simple Prompt with ChatGPT About Python Design Patterns

```
Describe 3 commonly used design patterns used by Python developers and why
those patterns are important
```

If you've had the opportunity to work at a company using Python professionally, then you've probably received a question very similar to the prompt above in an interview. The listing below is ChatGPT's response.

Listing 1-2. RESPONSE. ChatGPT's Response to the Prompt in Listing 1-1

Design patterns are standard solutions to common problems in software design, offering guidelines on how to structure your code in ways that make it more maintainable, scalable, and understandable. In Python development, certain design patterns are particularly favored due to the language's features and philosophy. Here are three commonly used design patterns among Python developers:

1. Singleton Pattern

Description: The Singleton Pattern ensures a class has only one instance and provides a global point of access to that instance. It's implemented in Python using a class that ensures only one instance of the class is created. The class stores the sole instance in a class variable, and any subsequent attempts to instantiate the class simply return the already existing instance.

Importance: The Singleton pattern is vital in scenarios where having multiple instances of a class could lead to problems, such as in the management of database connections or the configuration settings of an application. By ensuring only one instance is created, it prevents issues like inconsistent state or excessive resource usage.

2. Factory Method Pattern

Description: The Factory Method Pattern is a creational pattern that provides an interface for creating objects in a superclass but allows subclasses to alter the type of objects that will be created. Instead of calling a constructor directly, clients call the factory method, which can return an instance of different subclasses based on the input or the environment.

Importance: This pattern is important because it promotes loose coupling by eliminating the need to bind application-specific classes into your code. The factory method makes your code more modular, easier to extend, and

3

easier to maintain since the creation logic is encapsulated in the factory method. This is particularly useful in Python when dealing with a set of related objects that need to be created dynamically.

3. Observer Pattern

Description: The Observer Pattern defines a one-to-many dependency between objects so that when one object changes state, all its dependents are notified and updated automatically. It's typically implemented with a subject (or observable) object that holds a list of dependents (observers) and notifies them of any state changes, usually by calling one of their methods.

Importance: This pattern is crucial for creating event-driven applications or when changes in the state of one object may need to affect the state of other objects without tightly coupling them. It's widely used in GUI applications, real-time data monitoring, and event handling systems. The Observer pattern in Python helps in the development of responsive, decoupled systems that can react to changes dynamically.

These design patterns are important because they solve recurring design problems, making code more reusable, maintainable, and scalable. By using these patterns, Python developers can ensure their codebase is robust, efficient, and adaptable to change.

Not bad, huh? ChatGPT was not only able to provide a list of common design patterns used by Python developers but also explain valid reasons on why they are important – all done in natural language.

So, at the end of the day, what does this mean for Python developers? Well, it's actually a big deal. That's because developers are now able to create applications that can have some type of "understanding" of text in natural language. Before the advent of artificial intelligence (AI) tools like ChatGPT, developers typically had to create regular expressions (also called "regex") in order to perform rudimentary character and string pattern matching within a body of text. However, pattern matching and natural language understanding are two totally different things.

Regex vs. ChatGPT: Fight!

Note   If you already know that a regular expression can't perform natural language understanding or sentiment analysis, then feel free to skip this section.

I'm thoroughly convinced that every programmer somewhere in their lifetime has met *some guy* who happens to be an expert in writing regular expressions. Regular expressions are great because they serve the purpose of being able to parse large amounts of text in order to find patterns within the text programmatically.

However, one of the biggest downsides to regular expressions is that once they have been written, they are extremely difficult to read (in my opinion, even by the developer who originally wrote it).

So, let's see how regex holds up against ChatGPT, which has natural language processing (NLP) and natural language understanding (NLU) capabilities.

Listing 1-3 is a story of an impractically sad situation. However, it drives home the point that although regular expressions can be used to find words and phrases within a body of text, it can't be used to provide any type of NLU.

Listing 1-3. Sadstory.txt: A Sad Story About a Kid Who Didn't Eat Ice Cream

In the city of Buttersville,USA on Milkmaid street, there's a group of three friends: Marion Yogurt, Janelle de Queso, and Steve Cheeseworth III. On a hot summer's day, they heard the music from an ice cream truck, and decided to buy something to eat.

Marion likes strawberries, Janelle prefers chocolate, and Steve is lactose intolerant. That day, only two kids ate ice cream, and one of them bought a bottle of room-temperature water. The ice cream truck was fully stocked with the typical flavors of ice cream.

Analysis Question #1: Who Didn't Get Any Ice Cream, and Why?

Now, let's analyze this for a bit and ask some questions among ourselves. First of all, who didn't get any ice cream and why? The obvious answer is that Steve did not get any ice cream because of his lactose intolerance. However, since the story did not directly say that Steve did not buy ice cream, there's no way for a regular expression to match a text pattern in the story.

The regular expression could look for keywords such as "didn't have," "no ice cream," or the names of the kids. However, it would only be able to provide a response based on the presence of these patterns. For example, if the regular expression matches the pattern "didn't have" or "no ice cream" with Steve's name, it could show you the result of the text pattern. However, it certainly wouldn't be able to explain why Steve was the one who didn't have ice cream or provide any context-specific reasoning.

Now, let's provide the same story to ChatGPT, and ask the question, "Who didn't get any ice cream?" Listing 1-4, located below, takes our question and the story above and puts both together as a prompt.

Listing 1-4. PROMPT. The Sad Story Put into a Prompt

```
Using the information in the story below, who didn't get any ice cream
and why?
###
In the city of Buttersville,USA on Milkmaid street, there's a group of
three friends: Marion Yogurt, Janelle de Queso, and Steve Cheeseworth
III. On a hot summer's day, they heard the music from an ice cream truck,
and decided to buy something to eat.

Marion likes strawberries, Janelle prefers chocolate, and Steve is lactose
intolerant. That day, only two kids ate ice cream, and one of them bought
a bottle of room-temperature water. The ice cream truck was fully stocked
with the typical flavors of ice cream.
```

Notice how it is a best practice to provide some type of separation, in this case, "###", when creating a prompt (like the one above) where you have both instructions and data together. Later on, when we start using either the Playground or Python to programmatically invoke the ChatGPT API, you'll see that there's a much better way to provide that separation.

So, after sending the prompt, ChatGPT will provide you an answer like this.

Listing 1-5. RESPONSE. ChatGPT's Answer to Analysis Question #1

```
Based on the given information, Steve is lactose intolerant and therefore
cannot eat ice cream. Therefore, Steve is the one who didn't get any
ice cream.
```

As you can see, ChatGPT can utilize NLP and NLU, and therefore, it can understand (artificially intelligently, that is) the context of the scenario. It can interpret the relationships between the kids, their preferences, and Steve's lactose intolerance. It is able to understand that the last names of the children, the street name, and the city name are the names of dairy products but are obviously irrelevant to the question at hand.

Analysis Question #2: Which Kid Was Probably Left Sad?

Now, to further prove the point that a regular expression is unable to provide any type of NLP or NLU, let's use a new term called **sentiment analysis**. Therefore, after the ice cream truck drove away, which kid was left sad?

Since the story had no mention of any of the children's feelings or emotions, there is no text pattern that would allow any regular expression to return a match.

However, if you posed the same question to ChatGPT, it will return a response like this.

Listing 1-6. RESPONSE. ChatGPT's Answer to Analysis Question #2

```
Since Steve is lactose intolerant and cannot eat ice cream, he would be
the kid left sad because he couldn't enjoy the ice cream like Marion and
Janelle.
```

Therefore, ChatGPT is able to comprehend the scenario, reason through the information, and provide a correct answer along with an explanation for that answer.

7

Let's Unlearn Some Words in Order to Learn More About the ChatGPT API

First of all, before you get started working with the ChatGPT and OpenAI APIs, there are a few words and terms that you should be familiar with first; otherwise, things won't exactly make sense. So, let's make sure that we're all clear on the definition of models, prompts, tokens, and temperature when using ChatGPT programmatically.

Models. Models? Models!!!

As a Python developer, when you hear the term "model," you may immediately think of the representation of real-world entities in your Python app, right? For example, think of the term, "object model." Additionally, if you've ever worked with any type of database before, then the term "model" may *also* conjure into your mind the idea of the representation of data and their relationships in your database. For example, think of the term, "data model."

However, when working with the ChatGPT APIs (and artificial intelligence in general, for that matter), you need to forget both of those definitions, because they don't apply. In the realm of artificial intelligence, a "model" is a pre-trained **neural network**.

Remember, as I mentioned earlier, you won't need a PhD in machine learning in order to read this book. So, what's a neural network? Simply stated, a neural network is a fundamental component of artificial intelligence systems, because they are designed to simulate the way the human brain works by using interconnected layers of artificial neurons to process and analyze data. These networks can be trained on vast amounts of data to learn patterns and relationships and make predictions.

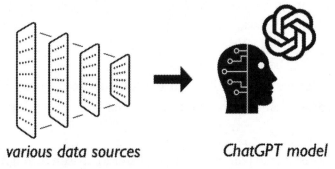

various data sources   ChatGPT model

Figure 1-1. *An AI Model Is Trained on Vast Amounts of Data*

In the context of AI, a "pre-trained model" refers to a neural network that has been trained on a specific task or dataset before being made available for use by developers. This training process involves exposing the model to large amounts of labeled and categorized (also called, "annotated") data and adjusting its internal parameters to optimize its performance on the given task.

Let's look at some of the models provided by OpenAI for developers to use to AI-enable their applications.

o1	The o1 series of large language models is trained through reinforcement learning to handle complex reasoning tasks. o1 models engage in deep thought before answering, generating a lengthy internal chain of reasoning prior to responding to the user. These models take a significantly longer time to generate a response than other models.
	Some o1 available models are:
	• o1
	• o1-mini
GPT-4	GPT-4 is one of the fastest generation of OpenAI's GPT set of models. GPT stands for generative pre-trained transformer, and these models have been trained to understand natural language as well as multiple programming languages. The GPT-4 models take text and images as inputs as the prompt and provide text as the output.
	Some of the GPT-4 models available are
	• gpt-4o
	• gpt-4o-mini
	• gpt-4o-realtime
	• gpt-4o-audio

(*continued*)

DALL·E	The DALL·E model can generate and edit images given a natural language prompt.
	Later in this book in Chapter 5, we're going to have some fun with the DALL·E model to visualize the conversation of what is being discussed in your favorite podcast episode.
	Some of the DALL·E models available are
	• dall-e-3 • dall-e-2
TTS	The TTS model takes text and converts it to audio with surprisingly good results. In most cases, the audio is almost indistinguishable from a human voice.
	Some of the TTS models available are
	• tts-1 • tts-1-hd
Whisper	Simply stated, the Whisper model converts audio into text.
	In this book, we're going to use the Whisper model to search for text in a podcast episode.
Embeddings	The Embeddings model can convert large amounts of text into a numerical representation of how the strings in the text are related. So how is that useful? Embeddings allow developers to do specific tasks using custom datasets. Yes, this means that you can train the Embeddings model on specific data that is relevant to your application. This allows you to do operations such as
	• Searching within your own body of text • Clustering data so that strings of text are grouped by their similarity • Getting recommendations (where items with related text strings are recommended) • Detecting anomalies (where outliers with little relatedness are identified) • Measuring diversity (where similarity distributions are analyzed) • Classifying data (where text strings are classified by their most similar label)

(continued)

Moderations	The Moderations models are fine-tuned models that can detect whether text may be sensitive or unsafe. These models can analyze text content and classify it according to the following categories: • Hate • Hate/threatening • Harassment • Harassment/threatening • Self-harm • Self-harm/intent • Self-harm/instructions • Sexual • Sexual/minors • Violence • Violence/graphic The Moderations models available are • text-moderation-latest • omni-moderation-latest • text-moderation-stable
Legacy and Deprecated	Since the debut of ChatGPT, OpenAI has continued to support their older AI models, but they have been labeled as "legacy" or "deprecated" models. These models continue to exist; however, they have released other models that are more accurate, faster, and cheaper to use.

Note   This is by no means an exhaustive list of models available for developers provided by OpenAI! As newer models are released, the older models will be marked as legacy or deprecated. Therefore, it's important to stay up-to-date by checking the list of available models on the OpenAI documentation list of models:

`https://platform.openai.com/docs/models`

When We Talk About Tokens, Don't Think About Access Tokens

When using a third party API, such as an external REST service, you might think of a "token" in the same sense as an access token, which is typically a UUID that allows you to identify yourself and maintain a session with the service. Well, forget that definition for now. Instead, when using the OpenAI APIs, a **token** is a chunk of a text that is approximately four characters long. That's it – nothing else special.

So, if a token is approximately a four-character chunk of text, then why do we care about it?

When working with the OpenAI textual models, developers need to be aware of token limitations, because they impact the cost and performance of API calls. For example, the gpt-4o and o1 models both support 128,000 tokens (which is approximately the size of a 300 page novel) that can go in your prompt. These input tokens are also called the **context windows**. In contrast, the maximum output tokens for gpt-4o is 16,384, while the maximum output tokens for the o1 model is 32,768.

As a result, developers need to take into account the length of the prompts as inputs and outputs to the models, ensuring that they fit within the model's token constraints.

Table 1-1 provides a list of some of the most current models with the token limitations and their pricing.

Table 1-1. *List of Models with Their Token Limitations and the Cost Per Token*

Model	Context Window	Cost of Token Input	Cost of Token Output
gpt-4o	128,000	$2.50 / 1M input tokens	$10.00 / 1M output tokens
gpt-4o-mini	128,000	$0.150 / 1M input tokens	$0.600 / 1M output tokens
o1	128,000	$15.00 / 1M input tokens	$60.00 / 1M output tokens
o1-mini	128,000	$3.00 / 1M input tokens	$12.00 / 1M output tokens

Temperature Is All About Creativity

Of course, ChatGPT isn't sentient, so it's incapable of thinking as we humans do. However, by adjusting the **temperature** setting in your prompts to the ChatGPT API, you can enable the responses to be more creative. Being aware of what it understands is crucial if you want to make best use of its potential.

Figure 1-2. *Modify the Temperature in Order to Get More (or Less) Creative Responses*

Getting Started with the OpenAI Playground

Now it's time to take the concepts that we've learned so far and start to put them to good use! However, we need to do first things first, and therefore, you will need to have a developer account with OpenAI and create an API key.

Head over to the following URL to create your dev account and API key:

https://platform.openai.com/account/api-keys

As you can see from Figure 1-3, you can name your API key anything that you want.

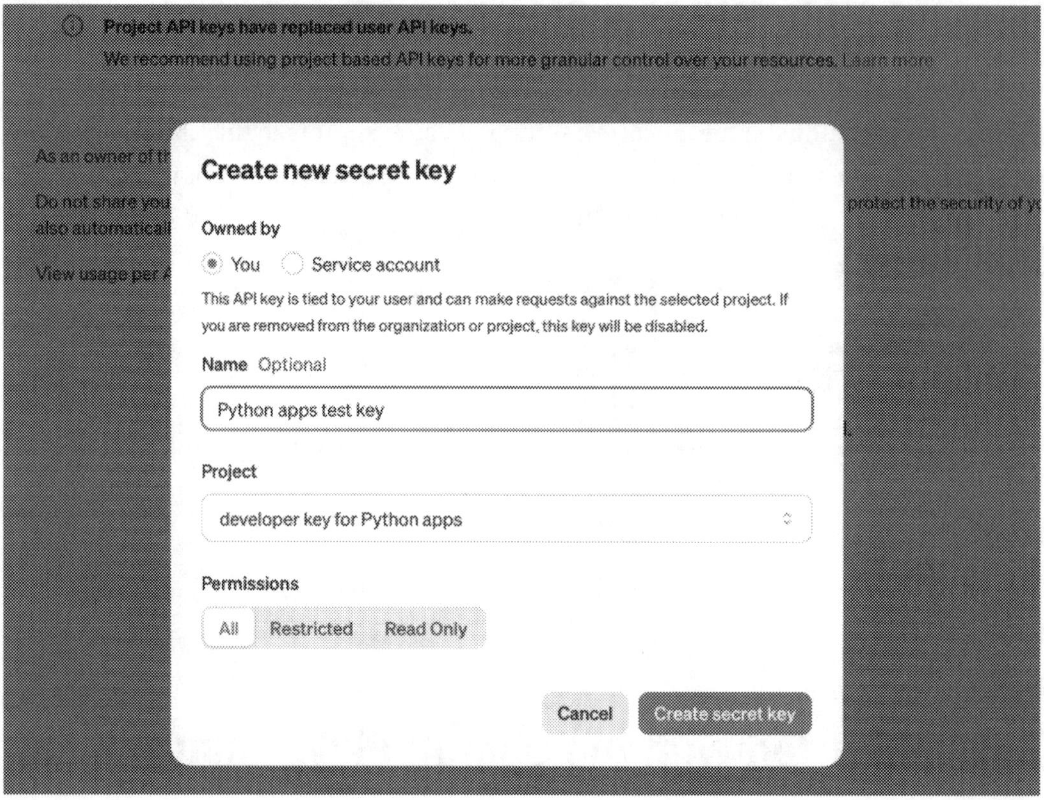

Figure 1-3. *Before You Can Access the Playground or Make API Calls, You Need to Have an API Key*

You should be aware that as a requirement to create an API key, you will need to provide to OpenAI a credit card so that you can be billed for usage of their models.

Now that you've got your API key, let's go straight to the Chat Playground at the following URL:

https://platform.openai.com/playground

Upon entering the Playground, click on the combobox at the top and select the Chat option to start the Chat Playground, as shown in Figure 1-4.

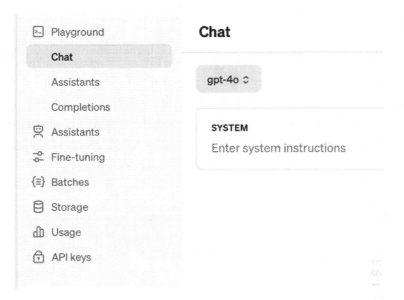

Figure 1-4. *After Entering the Playground, Select the Chat Option*

Figure 1-5 depicts the Chat Playground, with certain parts numbered so that they can be easily identified.

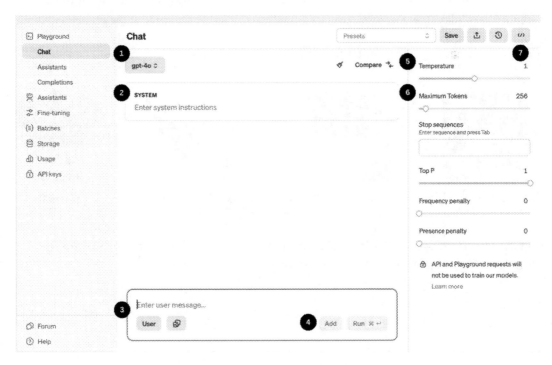

Figure 1-5. *The Chat Playground Can Be a Little Daunting at First Glance*

1. Model

Earlier in this chapter, we talked about the various models that are available for developers. Click the Model field in order to see a list of models that are available.

You may also see that some models have a month and day associated with their name, which is simply a snapshot of that model. Programmatically selecting a snapshot enables developers to have some sort of predictability in the responses that they will receive from ChatGPT, because the current models are always updated.

2. System

As you can see, the user interface for the Chat Playground is vastly more complex than the ChatGPT website that everyone else uses. So, let's talk about the **System** field (see Figure 1-5, item 2).

In my opinion, ChatGPT can be described as "a vastly powerful form of artificial intelligence...with amnesia." Therefore, when you're using ChatGPT programmatically, you need to inform the system who it is in the conversation!

Figure 1-6, shown below, gives you a glimpse of the thousands of different roles that ChatGPT can play in a conversation.

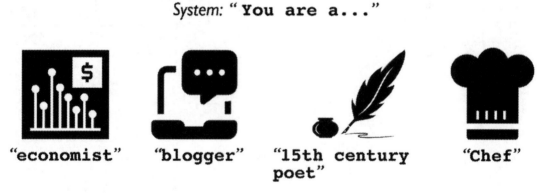

Figure 1-6. *The System Field in the Chat Playground Allows You to Set the Role That ChatGPT Will Play in the Conversation*

3. User/Assistant

The **User** field (Figure 1-5, item 3) in the Chat Playground is where you type your prompt to ChatGPT, which can be anything that you want, for example, "describe how telemedicine will affect the medical industry."

When you initially load the Chat Playground, the Assistant field is not visible. In order to make it appear, you need to click "User" button to switch to the Assistant field. Now, you may be asking yourself, "Why is this field needed at all?" Well, that's a fine question. If you want ChatGPT to remember something that it has already told you in a previous conversation, then you need to type into the **Assistant** field anything that it has already told you that you think is relevant in order to continue with the conversation. Remember, it is a vastly powerful AI, but it has amnesia!

4. Add (Optional)

Add (Figure 1-5, item 4) is where you'd click in order to add either an **Assistant** message to the conversation or another **User** message. Now, you may ask, "What's the point of adding yet another User message to the conversation, when I can type what I want in the original User field above?" Good question.

If you wanted to separate your command from your data, then you would use a separate **User** message for that.

Do you remember in Listing 1-4 earlier in this chapter, where we had to use the "###" to separate the command to ChatGPT from the data that we wanted it to analyze? Well, this is now no longer needed because the command would be the first **User** message; the data would be the second **User** message.

5. Temperature (Optional)

As noted earlier in this chapter, the temperature selector ranges between 0 and 2 and allows you to select the "randomness" of the response.

6. Maximum Tokens (Optional)

Do you remember the discussion earlier in this chapter about tokens? By selecting anything in the range for this item, you can adjust the number of tokens (which directly affects the number of words) in the response.

7. Code (Optional)

After you have submitted your prompt using the Playground, you can click on the **code** button (Figure 1-4, item 7) in order to see the code necessary to send the same prompt using any of the languages that they support.

Try It Now! Experimenting with the "System" Role

Now that we're familiar with several of the features of the Chat Playground, let's send our first prompt using the settings discussed above. Listings 1-7 and 1-8 below use the same prompt asking ChatGPT to give a few paragraphs on telemedicine, but the role of the system is vastly different from each other.

Listing 1-7. PROMPT. The Pros and Cons of Telemedicine as a Researcher

```
System: You are a strictly factual researcher
User: Write 3 paragraphs on pros and cons of telemedicine
```

Listing 1-8. PROMPT. The Pros and Cons of Telemedicine as an Opinionated Health Blogger

```
System: You are a highly opinionated health blogger who always has stories
with firsthand experience
User: Write 3 paragraphs on pros and cons of telemedicine
```

You are encouraged to try these two prompts yourself and see what the responses are. Adjust the settings for the temperature and token length to get familiar with how those parameters affect the outcome.

Conclusion

You just learned more about how ChatGPT can be used by developers. We covered some of the basics of the Chat Playground, which is a web interface for developers to interact with the ChatGPT API.

We talked about how to set the system, user, and assistant roles in the Chat Playground and how to adjust settings such as the temperature and maximum length of output.

You learned about some of the parameters and terminology necessary to use the Chat Playground, such as the model, temperature, and tokens. Getting familiar with the parameters of the Chat Playground is essential to knowing how to use the REST API since the Playground is a subset of capabilities offered by the REST API.

In the next chapter, we'll see how to use ChatGPT as your "pair-programmer" and create a productivity app that gives us weather and arrival time to work.

## CHAPTER 2

Using ChatGPT As Your Python Pair-Programmer

I'm a big fan of some of the practices of XP (eXtreme Programming) and especially pair-programming. No matter what flavor of pair-programming that you prefer, it involves two engineers sitting down at the same screen and solving the same problem together. One of the biggest benefits that you get is a fresh set of eyes on a problem, and of course, you now have two engineers who have "touched" the codebase instead of one. Sometimes you can have one engineer write the code and the other write the tests and the comments. No matter how you slice it, it's all good stuff.

Overview

This chapter will walk you through obtaining and testing out your API key, get you comfortable making calls to the OpenAI Python API for ChatGPT, and introduce you to how it's done for other models as well. Furthermore, we'll be using ChatGPT as a pair-programmer to get an application that will be able to receive the name of a city and the time you'd like to arrive to work, then give you the weather and an estimated arrival time based on traffic! Sounds exciting? Then, let's jump right in.

Installing (or Updating) the OpenAI Library with pip

In order to use the OpenAI library with Python, you will need at minimum Python 3.7.1 installed on your machine. In order to check the version of Python that you have, just open a terminal window, and execute:

```
python3 - v
```

© Lydia Evelyn, Bruce Hopkins 2024
L. Evelyn and B. Hopkins, *Beginning ChatGPT for Python*, https://doi.org/10.1007/979-8-8688-0929-3_2

If Python 3 is installed, then your terminal will display the version that you have. Now, of course, if your terminal is informing you that you have a noncompatible version (i.e., older than 3.7.1), then you should update Python on your machine. Additionally, if you don't have Python 3 installed at all, then you should install it before proceeding.

Now that you have all the prerequisites, it's time to install the OpenAI Python library itself. Go back to your terminal window, and execute the following command:

```
pip install --upgrade openai
```

The command above will install the OpenAI library for you if it doesn't already exist and will update the library to the most recent version if it's already there.

Three Ways to Set Your API Key

When setting up your API key for the OpenAI API, there are different methods to choose from, each designed for specific project needs and security concerns.

Option #1: Setting a System-Wide Environment Variable

The environment variable approach establishes a system-wide environment variable for API key storage. This provides a centralized point for key management, simplifying deployment across diverse projects.

Let's look at the steps on how we'd go about doing it.

For Mac OS

First off, open Terminal. You can find it in the applications folder or use spotlight (Command + Space) to search for it.

Next, edit your bash profile. For older MacOS versions, you'd use the command nano ~/.bash_profile. Users of newer MacOS versions will need to use nano ~/.zshrc. This will open the profile file in a text editor.

Now, let's add your environment variable. In the editor, add the line below, replacing 'your-api-key-here' with your actual API key without the single quotation marks.

```
export OPENAI_API_KEY='your-api-key-here'
```

CHAPTER 2   USING CHATGPT AS YOUR PYTHON PAIR-PROGRAMMER

Let's save and exit by pressing Ctrl+O to write the changes, then pressing Ctrl+X to close the editor.

Now, you're going to load your profile by using `source ~/.bash_profile` for older Mac OS versions and `source ~/.zshrc` for the newer Mac OS versions. This will load the updated profile.

Finally, we're going to verify that we've done everything correctly. In the terminal, type `echo $OPENAI_API_KEY`. If everything went well, it should display your API key, confirming the setup.

```
echo $OPENAI_API_KEY
```

For Windows

Start by opening the command prompt. You can find it by searching "cmd" in the start menu.

Now, we're going to set the environment variable in the current session by using the command below, replacing 'your-api-key-here' with your actual API key. This command sets the OPENAI_API_KEY for the current session.

```
setx OPENAI_API_KEY 'your-api-key-here'
```

You can make the setup permanent by adding the variable through system properties:

- Right-click "This PC" or "My Computer" and select "Properties."

- Click "Advanced system settings."

- Click the "Environment Variables" button.

- In the "System variables" section, click "New…" and enter `OPENAI_API_KEY` as the variable name and your API key as the variable value.

To make sure everything is working properly, reopen the command prompt and type the command below to verify the setup. It should display your API key.

```
echo %OPENAI_API_KEY%
```

For Linux

To set the environment variable for the current session, open a terminal window and use the export command. Replace 'your-api-key-here' with your actual API key.

```
export OPENAI_API_KEY='your-api-key-here'
```

To make the environment variable persistent across sessions, you can add it to your shell's configuration file, such as ~/.bashrc for Bash. Here's how you can do it:

Open the configuration file in a text editor. For example:

```
nano ~/.bashrc
```

Add the following line at the end of the file:

```
export OPENAI_API_KEY='your-api-key-here'
```

Save the file and exit the text editor.

To apply the changes immediately, you can either close and reopen the terminal or run:

```
source ~/.bashrc
```

To verify that the environment variable is set correctly, you can echo its value in the terminal. This command should display your API key:

```
echo $OPENAI_API_KEY
```

Option #2: Creating a .env File

Using a system-wide environment variable is great for making the API key accessible by any application or script running on the machine. However, if your use case is a little more simplistic, we can simply create a local variable accessible within just the scope of a particular program or script. It's also useful for situations in which different projects necessitate different keys, so you can prevent conflicts in key usage. Let's dive right in!

We're going to start by creating a local .env file. This file will house your API key, ensuring it's only utilized by the designated project. Navigate to the project folder where you intend to create the .env file.

Note   To prevent your .env file from being unintentionally shared via version control, create a .gitignore file in your project's root directory. Add a line with .env to ensure the confidentiality of your API key and other sensitive information.

Next, use the terminal or an IDE to create both the .gitignore and .env files. Copy your API key, and replace 'your-api-key-here' with your actual API key without the single quotation marks.

At this point, your .env file should look like this:

```
OPENAI_API_KEY='your-api-key-here'
```

Finally, you can import the API key into your Python code using the following snippet.

Listing 2-1. Importing Your .env File into Your Python Application

```
import os
from dotenv import load_dotenv
from openai import OpenAI

# Load environment variables from .env
load_dotenv()

# Use the API key from the environment variable
api_key = os.getenv("OPENAI_API_KEY")
client = OpenAI()
```

Option #3: Hard-Coding the API Key Directly in Your Application (Take with Caution)

This last method isn't recommended for long-term use because of security reasons. But, for the sake of knowing how it works, we're going to cover how you can hard-code your API key into your application if you want to quickly test out your API key to make sure it's working.

To begin, you'll assign the API key to a variable within the Python code. Replace "YOUR_API_KEY" with the actual API key you received from OpenAI. Ensure that this API key is kept secure and not shared publicly.

Next, you'll initialize the OpenAI client within your Python script. This is done by instantiating the OpenAI class with the api_key parameter set to the API key. By providing the API key during initialization, you enable the OpenAI client to access the services offered by the OpenAI API. This step ensures that your Python script can communicate with the OpenAI API using the specified API key.

Listing 2-2. Coding Your API Key Directly into Your Application

```
from openai import OpenAI

# API key
API_KEY = "your-api-key-here"

# Initialize OpenAI client with hardcoded API key
client = OpenAI(api_key=API_KEY)
```

Now, let's make our first application with the OpenAI API, and test out the key at the same time by getting a list of models useable with the OpenAI API.

Note   From this point on, the code examples will be accessing our API key with a local .env file.

Creating Your First Python ChatGPT App: `model_lister.py`

We're actually going to accomplish two tasks at once here. We're going to create a basic application in Python using the OpenAI APIs, and in the process, we're going to verify that we've properly obtained an API key. So, needless to say, in case you haven't done so already, follow the instructions in Chapter 1 to create your OpenAI developer account and obtain your API key. Going forward, all the code samples in this book require a valid API key.

Using `OpenAI.models.list()` to Get a List of Available Models

One of the most basic (but also essential) capabilities that we can invoke is in the Model class. Why, you may ask? The Model class allows you to get a list of all the AI models that are currently available for use by developers via the Python API.

After successfully getting an instance of the OpenAI and Model objects, the API will provide what is referred to within the OpenAI API as a "SyncPage," which is essentially a dictionary with the structure shown in Table 2-1.

Handling the Response

Table 2-1. *The Structure of the Model Object*

Field	Type	Description
object	String	This always returns the literal "list."
data	Dictionary	A dictionary of AI models offered by OpenAI.
↳ id	String	The unique ID of the AI model, which is essentially the full name of the model.
↳ object	String	This always returns the literal "model."
↳ created	Integer	The creation date for the model.
↳ owned_by	String	The name of the organization that owns the model.

Note   Since objects can contain dictionaries (which can be hard to represent in a table), we're using the following notation " ↳ " to indicate the elements of the dictionary. As you can see from Table 2-1, "id," "object," "created," and "owned_by" are all elements of the "data" dictionary in the response.

Now that we have the details of the Model object, let's talk about how we can test the API key we obtained in the first chapter. There are actually a few ways to do this.

Using Your API Key to Get a List of Available Models with the OpenAI API

With our API key set up in a local .env file, we're going to use the following code to get a list of models available within the OpenAI API, which will then be printed into our terminal.

Listing 2-3. Getting a List of Models Available with the OpenAI API by Calling the `models.list()` method with `model_lister.py`

```
"""Module for interacting with OpenAI API to list the models available"""

import os
from dotenv import load_dotenv
from openai import OpenAI

# Load environment variables from .env
load_dotenv()

# Use the API key from the environment variable
api_key = os.getenv("OPENAI_API_KEY")
client = OpenAI()

models_list = client.models.list()

print(models_list)
```

After running the code in Listing 2-3, Listing 2-4 is a truncated response that you should expect to see.

Listing 2-4. An Ugly-Looking Response After Running Our model_lister.py Application

```
SyncPage[Model](data=[Model(id='dall-e-3', created=1698785189,
object='model', owned_by='system'), Model(id='dall-e-2',
created=1698798177, object='model', owned_by='system'), Model(id='gpt-3.5-
turbo-0125', created=1706048358, object='model', owned_by='system'),
Model(id='text-embedding-ada-002', created=1671217299, object='model',
owned_by='openai-internal'), Model(id='tts-1-hd-1106', created=1699053533,
object='model', owned_by='system'), Model(id='tts-1-hd',
created=1699046015, object='model', owned_by='system'). . .
```

Getting a Prettier List of Models

Listing 2-4 is a partial list due to the sheer size of the number of models available for developers to use! The good news, however, is that the full response is provided as a table in Appendix 1.

So, first off, this is great. We know that our API key works! However, if you hadn't noticed, we're getting a fairly ugly-looking response. For the sake of brevity, Listing 2-4 has been shortened, but it's quite obvious no one is going to want to read that big ol' chunk of text when we just want to know all of the models within the OpenAI API.

It would be nice if we could get a more cleaned up response after running our code. So, let's add some code that will format the response.

Listing 2-5. Cleaning Up the Response We Get from the OpenAI API with `model_lister_pretty.py`

```python
"""Module for interacting with OpenAI API to list the models available"""

import os
from dotenv import load_dotenv
from openai import OpenAI

# Load environment variables from .env
load_dotenv()

# Use the API key from the environment variable
api_key = os.getenv("OPENAI_API_KEY")
client = OpenAI()

models_list = client.models.list()

# Iterate through the list and print model information
for model in models_list.data:
    print(f"Model ID: {model.id}")
    print(f"Created: {model.created}")
    print(f"Object: {model.object}")
    print(f"Owned By: {model.owned_by}")
    print("\n=============================\n")   # Separator for better
                                                 readability
```

Listing 2-6 has the response from running `model_lister_pretty.py`.

Listing 2-6. The Cleaned Up Response from OpenAI with `model_lister_pretty.py`

```
Model ID: text-embedding-ada-002
Created: 1671217299
Object: model
Owned By: openai-internal


=====================================================


Model ID: gpt-3.5-turbo-instruct
Created: 1692901427
Object: model
Owned By: system


=====================================================


Model ID: dall-e-3
Created: 1698785189
Object: model

Owned By: system
```

Wait, How Many Tokens Are in My Prompt?

At a certain point, you're going to start thinking about the prompts that you plan to
send to ChatGPT and give considerable thought to the token limitations (and the costs)
regarding the model that you want to use. In case you forgot, be sure to refer back to
Table 1-1 for a list of models and the price of the tokens. Additionally, OpenAI created
a simple-to-use website that allows you to see how many tokens are in your prompt, as
shown in the figure below.

ChatGPT Token Counter

https://platform.openai.com/tokenizer

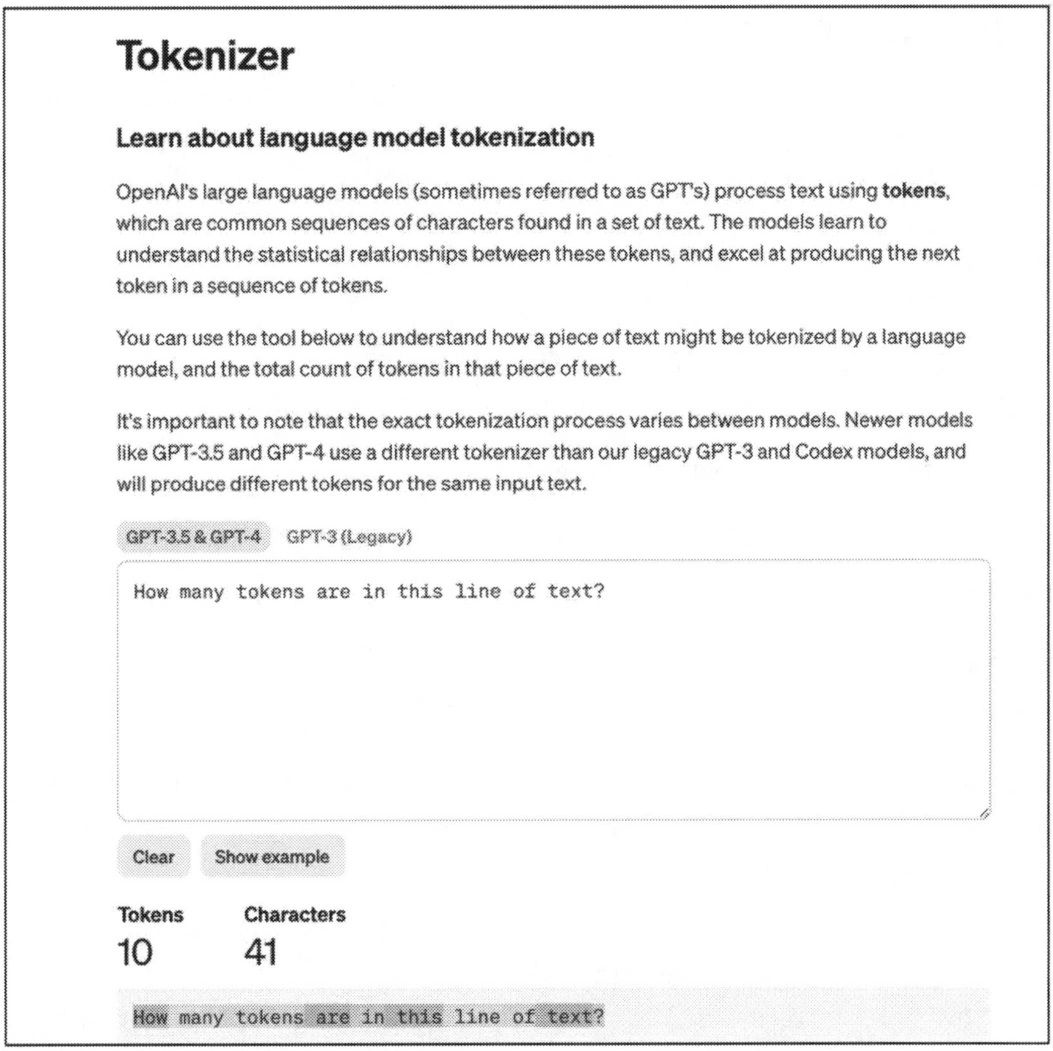

Tokenizer

Learn about language model tokenization

OpenAI's large language models (sometimes referred to as GPT's) process text using **tokens**, which are common sequences of characters found in a set of text. The models learn to understand the statistical relationships between these tokens, and excel at producing the next token in a sequence of tokens.

You can use the tool below to understand how a piece of text might be tokenized by a language model, and the total count of tokens in that piece of text.

It's important to note that the exact tokenization process varies between models. Newer models like GPT-3.5 and GPT-4 use a different tokenizer than our legacy GPT-3 and Codex models, and will produce different tokens for the same input text.

| GPT-3.5 & GPT-4 | GPT-3 (Legacy) |

How many tokens are in this line of text?

Clear   Show example

Tokens   **Characters**
10   41

How many tokens are in this line of text?

Figure 2-1. *The ChatGPT Tokenizer Can Give You a Quick Count of the Tokens in Your Prompt*

Using ChatGPT As a Pair-Programmer to Build a Weather Application

Now that we've made sure that our API key works, it's time to start writing our first project with ChatGPT. This is the exciting part! We're going to use ChatGPT to help us create an application in Python that will give us the weather and the time it'll take us to get to work from the location of our home to work. Sounds impressive, doesn't it?

Setting Up the Prompt

Let's ask ChatGPT how we should get started. Now is a good time to practice prompt engineering. We're going to explain to ChatGPT what we want and see what it comes up with. This is the prompt we used.

Listing 2-7. Prompting ChatGPT to Help Us Make a Weather App For Productivity

```
How can I make a simple application in Python that allows me to type in my
city and then use AccuWeather's API to give me the weather?
```

This is the code we got in the response.

Listing 2-8. Getting a Response Back from ChatGPT to Build Our Weather App, accuweather_forecaster.py

```
To create a simple application in Python that allows you to type in your
city and retrieve the weather using AccuWeather's API, you can follow
these steps:

    - Sign up for an AccuWeather API key on their developer portal:
      https://developer.accuweather.com/.
    - Install the requests library if you haven't already. You can install
      it via pip:

pip install requests

    - Write a Python script to interact with the AccuWeather API. Here's a
      basic example:

import requests

def get_weather(accuweather_api_key, city):
    base_url = "http://dataservice.accuweather.com/locations/v1/
    cities/search"
    params = {
```

```python
        "apikey": accuweather_api_key,
        "q": city,
    }
    response = requests.get(base_url, params=params)
    location_data = response.json()
    if location_data:
        location_key = location_data[0]["Key"]
        weather_url = f"http://dataservice.accuweather.com/current
                      conditions/v1/{location_key}"
        params = {
            "apikey": accuweather_api_key,
        }
        response = requests.get(weather_url, params=params)
        weather_data = response.json()
        if weather_data:
            weather_text = weather_data[0]["WeatherText"]
            temperature = weather_data[0]["Temperature"]["Metric"]["Value"]
            print(f"The current weather in {city} is {weather_text} with a
            temperature of {temperature}°C.")
        else:
            print("Weather data not found.")
    else:
        print("Location not found.")

if __name__ == "__main__":
    accuweather_api_key = "api-key"
    city = input("Enter your city: ")
    get_weather(accuweather_api_key, city)
```

Creating accuweather_forecaster.py with the AccuWeather API

So, let's follow the steps we got from ChatGPT. First, we need to set up an account with AccuWeather. Go to https://developer.accuweather.com/ and hit register to sign up.

Figure 2-2. AccuWeather Home Page for Developers

After signing in, you'll notice that the menu changes, and you can now navigate over to **My Apps**.

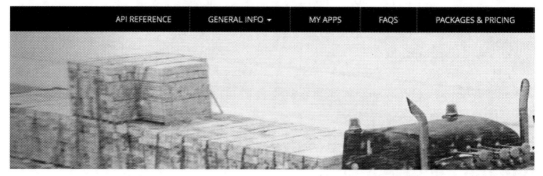

Figure 2-3. Navigating to the My Apps Tab on the AccuWeather Developer Portal

Once you're on the **My Apps** tab, you're going to want to **Add a new App** in order to get an API key to use in our application.

Figure 2-4. *Creating a New App with AccuWeather*

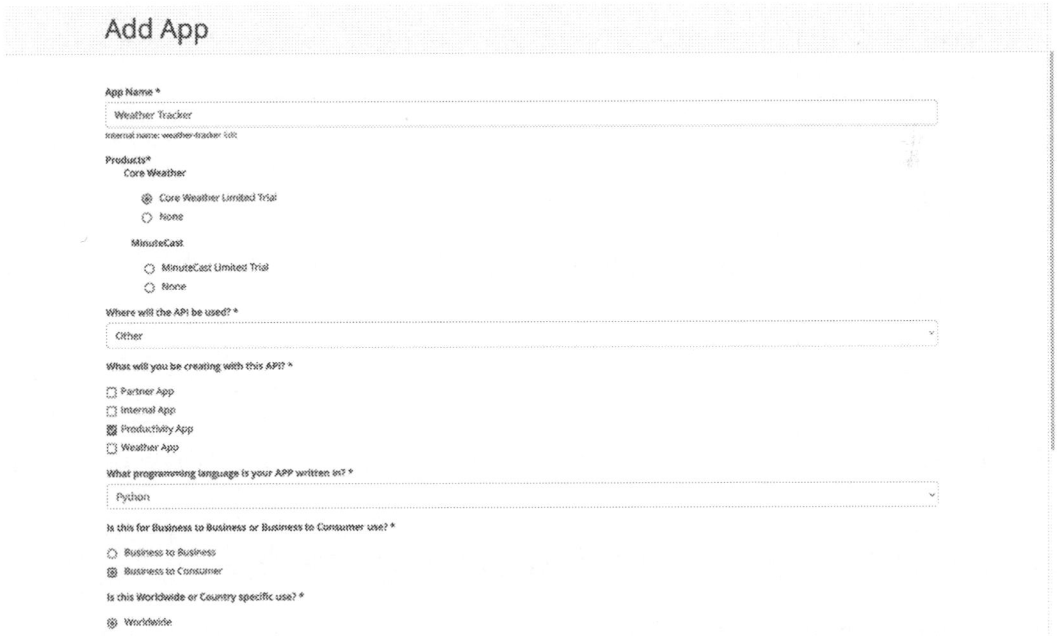

Add App

App Name *

Weather Tracker

Internal name: weather-tracker Edit

Products*
Core Weather

⊙ Core Weather Limited Trial
○ None

MinuteCast

○ MinuteCast Limited Trial
○ None

Where will the API be used? *

Other   ⌄

What will you be creating with this API? *

☐ Partner App
☐ Internal App
☑ Productivity App
☐ Weather App

What programming language is your APP written in? *

Python   ⌄

Is this for Business to Business or Business to Consumer use? *

○ Business to Business
⊙ Business to Consumer

Is this Worldwide or Country specific use? *

⊙ Worldwide

Figure 2-5. *Adding Specifications for Our AccuWeather App*

As you set things up, you'll need to name your app and answer benign questions like where the API will be used and what you plan to be creating with the API. As you can see in Figure 2-5, we've called our AccuWeather app "Weather Tracker"; however, this is not the name of our actual Python application, `accuweather_forecaster.py`.

The names don't have to match. You can name your app in AccuWeather whatever you like. The most important configuration to enable here is where you're being asked to specify the product you're intending to use. **Be sure to enable the Core Weather Limited Trial.**

The difference between choosing Core Weather and MinuteCast is an application that works and an application that doesn't and takes a long time to figure out why it doesn't (can you tell this was a memorable experience?).

It may take some time for your application to be approved, but usually, this is a very quick process. When it's done, you'll see your new application on the **My Apps** page, which will include your API key! Mission accomplished.

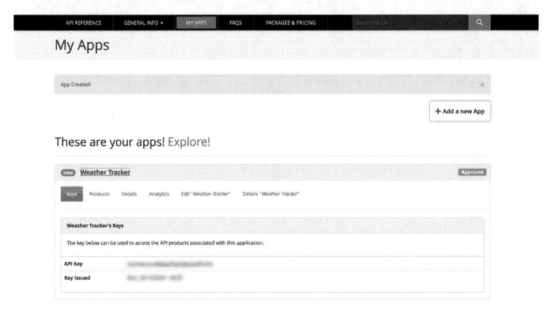

Figure 2-6. *Seeing Your Newly Created App on the AccuWeather Developer Portal*

Refining Our Prompt with Prompt Engineering

Back to our code example provided by ChatGPT, we can provide our API key where it's required in the code. For clarity's sake, we've renamed the API key variable to "`accuweather_api_key`." If you need a refresher, this is the line of code where we need to input our API key from AccuWeather.

Listing 2-9. Inputting Our API Key from AccuWeather into Our `accuweather_` `forecaster.py` app

```
if __name__ == "__main__":
    accuweather_api_key = "your-accuweather-api-key-here"
    city = input("Enter your city: ")
    get_weather(accuweather_api_key, city)
```

Now, with everything all together, when you run the code, you should see a prompt that asks you to input the name of a city.

Listing 2-10. After Running the Script, Enter a Valid City Name

```
Enter your city:
```

Once you provide a valid city name, you should find that everything runs smoothly and, you'll get a response that looks something like this (obviously, the forecast will change depending on what city you decide to enter and, well, what the weather is like the day you run it).

Listing 2-11. It Was a Little Chilly in New York City on the Day We Ran the `accuweather_forecaster.py` Script

```
The current weather in New York City is Sunny with a temperature of 5.6°C.
```

We get a nice, basic description of the weather in New York City from running the code, but there are a couple of things we can improve on.

AccuWeather has icons for various weather conditions. Right now, we can see that the weather in New York is currently sunny, but we could also get a longer description that describes the weather for the rest of the day. Americans might also prefer to see the temperature in Fahrenheit (as American authors, that's what we're going to choose as well). So, let's get ChatGPT to help us make those changes.

So that ChatGPT can retain the context, we're going to prompt ChatGPT in the same Chat conversation as follows.

Listing 2-12. Prompting ChatGPT to Help Change the Code in Our
`accuweather_forecaster.py` Application to Get a More Detailed Response from
the AccuWeather API

```
This code works, however, I'd like to make the following changes:

- get the temperature in Fahrenheit
- make an API call to get an icon number and an icon url to print in the
  response
- make an API call to get a weather description in the response
```

This is the answer we got from ChatGPT.

Listing 2-13. Response from ChatGPT to Modify the Code in Our `accuweather_`
`forecaster.py` Application

```
Sure, here's the modified version of the code to accommodate your
requirements:

```python

import requests

def get_weather(accuweather_api_key, city):
    base_url = "http://dataservice.accuweather.com/locations/v1/
    cities/search"
    params = {
        "apikey": accuweather_api_key,
        "q": city,
    }
    response = requests.get(base_url, params=params)
    location_data = response.json()
    if location_data:
        location_key = location_data[0]["Key"]
```
```

```python
    weather_url = f"http://dataservice.accuweather.com/
    currentconditions/v1/{location_key}"
    params = {
        "apikey": accuweather_api_key,
    }
    response = requests.get(weather_url, params=params)
    weather_data = response.json()
    if weather_data:
        weather_text = weather_data[0]["WeatherText"]
        temperature_imperial = weather_data[0]["Temperature"]
        ["Imperial"]["Value"]

        # Fetching icon number and icon URL
        icon_number = weather_data[0]["WeatherIcon"]
        icon_url = f"http://developer.accuweather.com/sites/default/
        files/{icon_number:02d}-s.png"

        # Making API call to get weather headline
        headline_url = f"http://dataservice.accuweather.com/forecasts/
        v1/daily/1day/{location_key}"
        response = requests.get(headline_url, params=params)
        headline_data = response.json()
        if headline_data and "Headline" in headline_data:
            headline_text = headline_data["Headline"]["Text"]
            print(f"The current weather in {city} is {weather_text}
            with a temperature of {temperature_imperial}°F.")
            print(f"Weather Headline: {headline_text}")
            print(f"Weather Icon: {icon_url}")
        else:
            print("Weather headline not found.")
    else:
        print("Weather data not found.")
else:
    print("Location not found.")
```

```
if __name__ == "__main__":
    accuweather_api_key = "your-accuweather-api-key-here"
    city = input("Enter your city: ")
    get_weather(accuweather_api_key, city)
```

This modified version of the code:

Converts temperature from Celsius to Fahrenheit.

Retrieves weather icon number and description.

Prints the weather icon number and constructs the icon URL.

Make sure to replace "your-accuweather-api-key-here" with your actual AccuWeather API key.

When we run this code, we get exactly what we were looking for. We'll enter a valid city name again (New York City, in our case), and this is the response we got.

Listing 2-14. Response from the AccuWeather API After Running the Modified Code in Our accuweather_forecaster API Key

```
Weather in New York City:
Temperature: 45.0°F
Weather Text: Sunny
Weather Headline: Expect rainy weather late tomorrow night through late
Thursday night
Icon Number: 1
Icon URL: http://developer.accuweather.com/sites/default/files/01-s.png
```

Now, our code works exactly the way we want it to, but there's even more room for improvement. If you're using an IDE with any kind of linting, you might see quite a few linting errors from the code we're running now. These are some of the linting errors you might see with the code as it is now.

Listing 2-15. The Linting Errors Pointed Out by Our IDE

```
Redefining name 'city' from outer scope (line 45)
Redefining name 'city' from outer scope (line 45)
Missing timeout argument for method 'requests.get' can cause your program
to hang indefinitely
```

```
Missing timeout argument for method 'requests.get' can cause your program
to hang indefinitely
Missing timeout argument for method 'requests.get' can cause your program
to hang indefinitely
Missing module docstring
Missing function or method docstring
Line too long (102/100)
Line too long (103/100)
Line too long (121/100)
Constant name "accuweather_api_key" doesn't conform to UPPER_CASE
naming style
```

Note   So, what exactly is linting? Linting is the process of analyzing code for errors, but it's mostly for stylistic inconsistencies. It helps maintain code quality, enforces coding standards, and helps make code more readable by using common conventions.

To clean this up, we're just going to run this by ChatGPT, again, in the same Chat conversation.

Listing 2-16. Prompting ChatGPT to Help Us Resolve Our Linting Errors

```
My IDE is making me aware of the following linting errors. Help me modify
my code to comply to the styling standards.

###

Redefining name 'city' from outer scope (line 45)
Redefining name 'city' from outer scope (line 45)
Missing timeout argument for method 'requests.get' can cause your program
to hang indefinitely
Missing timeout argument for method 'requests.get' can cause your program
to hang indefinitely
Missing timeout argument for method 'requests.get' can cause your program
to hang indefinitely
Missing module docstring
```

Missing function or method docstring
Line too long (102/100)
Line too long (103/100)
Line too long (121/100)
Constant name "accuweather_api_key" doesn't conform to UPPER_CASE
naming style

This was the response we got from ChatGPT.

Listing 2-17. Getting a Response from ChatGPT That Resolves All of Our Linting
Errors in accuweather_forecaster_cleaned_up.py

To address the linting errors and improve the code's compliance with
styling standards, you can make the following modifications:

- Add module docstring to describe the purpose of the script.
- Add function docstring to describe the purpose of the `get_weather`
  function.
- Rename the `accuweather_api_key` variable to `ACCUWEATHER_API_KEY` to
  comply with the UPPER_CASE naming convention for constants.
- Remove redefining `city` from the outer scope by renaming the input
  parameter of the `get_weather` function.
- Add a timeout argument to the `requests.get` calls to prevent hanging
  indefinitely.
- Split long lines to comply with the maximum line length.

Here's the modified code:

```python
"""

Script to fetch current weather information using AccuWeather API.
"""

import requests
```

```python
def get_weather(accuweather_api_key, city):
    """

    Get current weather information for a given city using AccuWeather API.

    Args:
        accuweather_api_key (str): AccuWeather API key.
        city (str): Name of the city for which weather information is
        requested.

    Returns:
        None
    """
    base_url = "http://dataservice.accuweather.com/locations/v1/
    cities/search"
    params = {
        "apikey": accuweather_api_key,
        "q": city,
    }
    response = requests.get(base_url, params=params, timeout=10)
    location_data = response.json()
    if location_data:
        location_key = location_data[0]["Key"]
        weather_url = f"http://dataservice.accuweather.com/
        currentconditions/v1/{location_key}"
        params = {
            "apikey": accuweather_api_key,
        }
        response = requests.get(weather_url, params=params, timeout=10)
        weather_data = response.json()
        if weather_data:
            weather_text = weather_data[0]["WeatherText"]
            temperature_imperial = weather_data[0]["Temperature"]
            ["Imperial"]["Value"]

            # Fetching icon number and icon URL
            icon_number = weather_data[0]["WeatherIcon"]
            icon_url = (
```

```python
                    f"http://developer.accuweather.com/sites/default/files/"
                    f"{icon_number:02d}-s.png"
                )

                # Making API call to get weather headline
                headline_url = (
                    f"http://dataservice.accuweather.com/forecasts/v1/"
                    f"daily/1day/"
                    f"{location_key}"
                )
                response = requests.get(headline_url, params=params,
                timeout=10)
                headline_data = response.json()
                if headline_data and "Headline" in headline_data:
                    headline_text = headline_data["Headline"]["Text"]
                    print(f"The current weather in {city} is {weather_text} "
                            f"with a temperature of {temperature_imperial}°F.")
                    print(f"Weather Headline: {headline_text}")
                    print(f"Weather Icon: {icon_url}")
                else:
                    print("Weather headline not found.")
            else:
                print("Weather data not found.")
        else:
            print("Location not found.")

if __name__ == "__main__":
    ACCUWEATHER_API_KEY = "your-accuweather-api-key"
    user_city = input("Enter your city: ")
    get_weather(ACCUWEATHER_API_KEY, user_city)
```
```

These modifications should address the linting errors and improve the code's readability and compliance with styling standards. Be sure to replace "your-accuweather-api-key-here" with your actual API key.
```

Using ChatGPT As a Pair-Programmer to Build an Application That Estimates Distance and Arrival Time

The next thing we're going to want to do is start making an application that can give us an arrival time and distance from one place to another, for example, from our house to our workplace. We're going to use a classic here and dive into the Google Maps API.

Creating a Project with Google Maps Platform API

Most people already have a Gmail account, but on the off chance you don't, be sure to create one before proceeding.

Google has a mountain of APIs for various applications, so we're going to need to go directly to the API for Google Maps, in specific, at `https://developers.google.com/maps/documentation`.

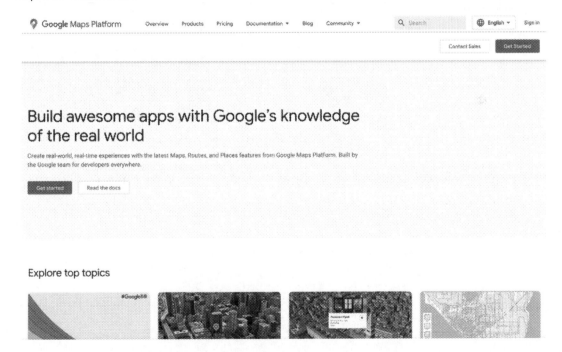

Figure 2-7. *The Google Maps Platform Home Page*

On the Google Maps Platform page, click **Getting Started** to set up your account for using the APIs. After following the steps Google presents you with, you'll be taken to the page on Figure 2-8, where you can see the different APIs available with the Google Maps Platform. But what'll probably catch your attention first is the fact that you still have to **Finish Account Setup**.

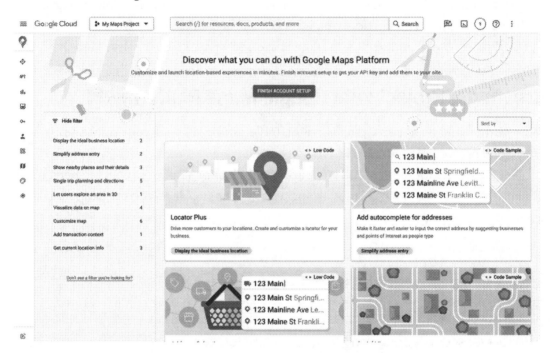

Figure 2-8. *Finishing Your Google Maps Platform Account Setup*

Finishing your account setup will compose of entering credit card information so you can start the free trial that will allow you $200 worth of credit, which is more than enough for the purposes of our testing.

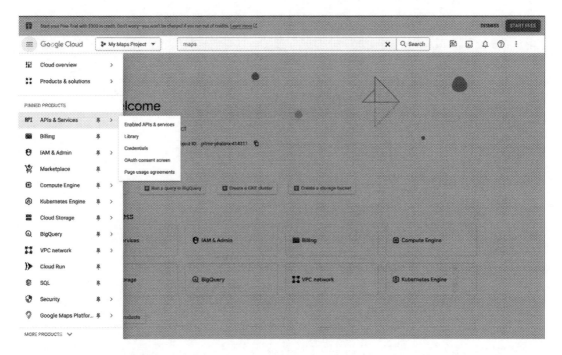

Figure 2-9. *Navigating to the APIs & Services Tab on the Google Maps Platform*

After properly setting up your account, you'll be greeted by a welcome page. On the left, you'll find a menu icon you can click on to reveal a list of services you have access to. You want to navigate to **Apps & Services** and then click **Library**.

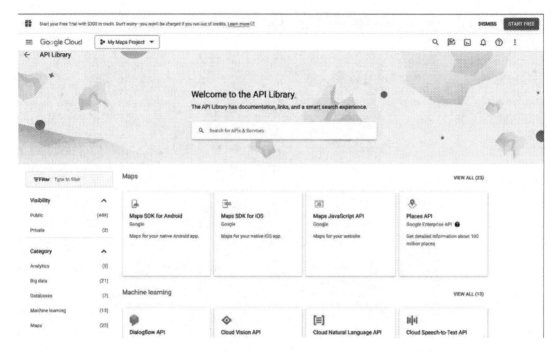

Figure 2-10. *The API Library Page*

You're going to want to click on **Maps JavaScript API** and then **Enable** it.

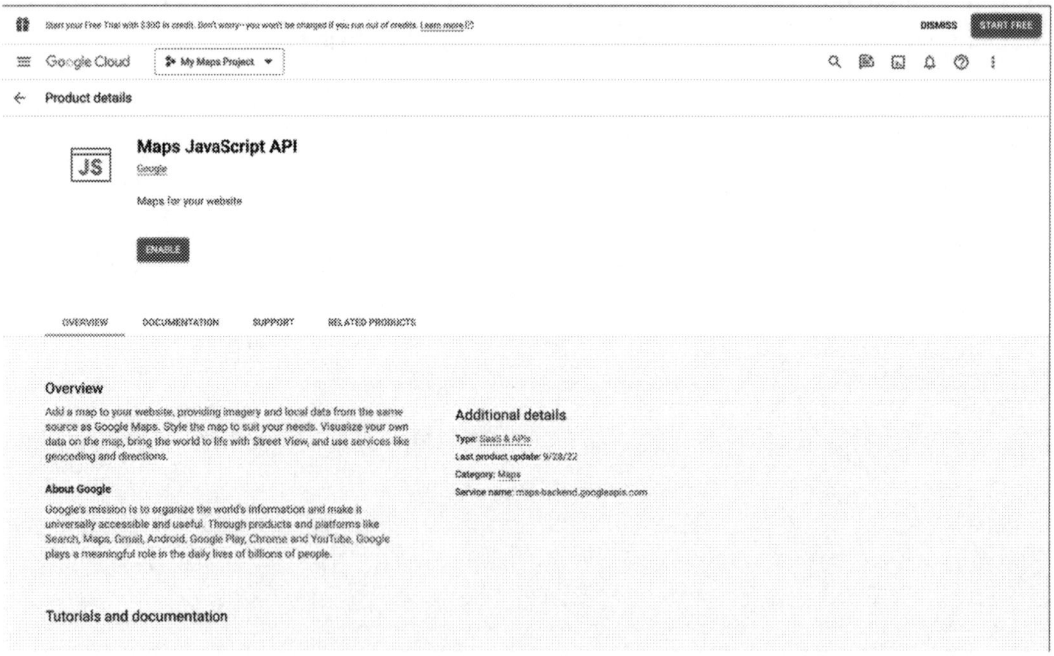

Figure 2-11. *Enabling the JavaScript API*

After enabling the JavaScript API, go back twice and open the menu again, and then click on the **Google Maps Platform** to see the dashboard for Google Maps.

From here, we're going to be looking at another side menu that looks similar to the one from before, but here we're going to click on **Apps & Services** again to see a different page this time. From here, you can click on **Routes** to enable it.

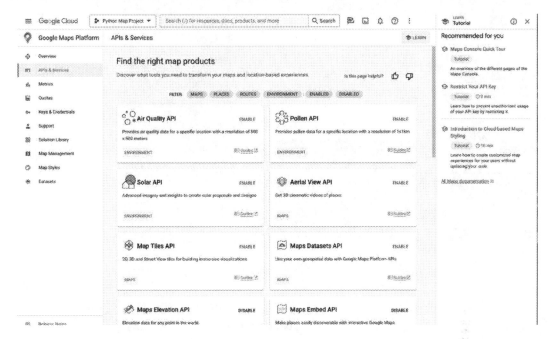

Figure 2-12. *Enabling the Routes API*

Once you've enabled the API we need, navigate to the **Keys & Credentials** tab and **Create a new API key**.

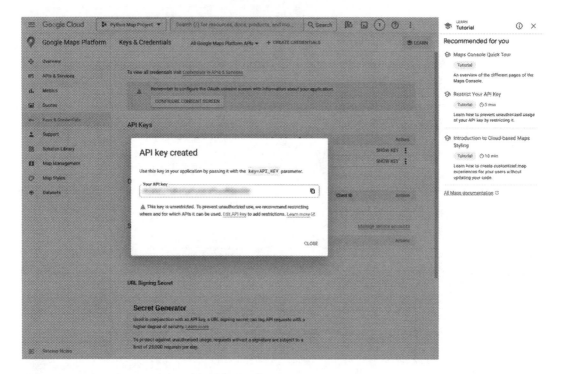

Figure 2-13. *The Keys and Credentials Page on the Google Maps Platform*

Now that we have our Google Maps API key, we can make use of our pair programmer. There are actually two ways we can use ChatGPT to make it easier to run code that successfully retrieves the information we want: how far away is the destination and how long will it take to get there (and here's a fun fact – the Google Maps Routes API factors in traffic trends in the estimated travel time, making our application perfect for productivity!).

Using ChatGPT to Take a cURL Command and Make It Useable in Python: The Flexible Programmer's Approach

To some, using cURL can be a bit intimidating, which is why we've laid out two methods for using ChatGPT to help us write code that makes use of the Google Maps Platform API; one way that takes cURL code and "translates" it to something we can use in Python and another way that surpasses the need to look at any scary cURL code at all.

In this first method, instead of navigating the Google Maps Platform documentation, we're actually going to cut to the chase and give you the cURL code you need and show you how to use ChatGPT to make it useable to you as a Python programmer. You're welcome.

Here's the cURL code from the Google Maps Platform documentation.

Listing 2-18. cURL Code for Using the Google Maps Routes API

```
curl -X POST -d '{
  "origin":{
    "location":{
      "latLng":{
        "latitude": 37.419734,
        "longitude": -122.0827784
      }
    }
  },
  "destination":{
    "location":{
      "latLng":{
        "latitude": 37.417670,
        "longitude": -122.079595
      }
    }
  },
  "travelMode": "DRIVE",
  "routingPreference": "TRAFFIC_AWARE",
  "departureTime": "2023-10-15T15:01:23.045123456Z",
  "computeAlternativeRoutes": false,
  "routeModifiers": {
    "avoidTolls": false,
    "avoidHighways": false,
    "avoidFerries": false
  },
  "languageCode": "en-US",
  "units": "IMPERIAL"
}' \
-H 'Content-Type: application/json' -H 'X-Goog-Api-Key: YOUR_API_KEY' \
-H 'X-Goog-FieldMask: routes.duration,routes.distanceMeters,routes.
polyline.encodedPolyline' \
'https://routes.googleapis.com/directions/v2:computeRoutes'
```

Remember, when practicing prompt engineering, the best practice is to separate the instructions from the content with three hashes (###) to get the best results. To that end, here's the prompt we gave ChatGPT so that we could use this cURL code and produce the results we desired using three hashes to separate the instructions from the content, the content being the cURL code presented in Listing 2-18:

Listing 2-19. Prompting ChatGPT to Provide Python Code Using the cURL Command As Context

```
I'm coding in Python and trying to build an application that makes a
request to the Google Maps API and pulls down the amount of time it'll
take to get from one location to the other. This is the cURL code that
would accomplish that goal. Help me convert this to something I can use
in Python.
###
[cURL code from listing 2-18]
```

This is the code we got in the response from ChatGPT.

Listing 2-20. Getting a Response Back from ChatGPT with Useable Python Code

```python
import requests
import json

# Define the payload
payload = {
    "origin": {
        "location": {
            "latLng": {
                "latitude": 37.419734,
                "longitude": -122.0827784
            }
        }
    },
```

```python
    "destination": {
        "location": {
            "latLng": {
                "latitude": 37.417670,
                "longitude": -122.079595
            }
        }
    },
    "travelMode": "DRIVE",
    "routingPreference": "TRAFFIC_AWARE",
    "departureTime": "2025-02-17T17:00:00Z",
    "computeAlternativeRoutes": False,
    "routeModifiers": {
        "avoidTolls": False,
        "avoidHighways": False,
        "avoidFerries": False
    },
    "languageCode": "en-US",
    "units": "IMPERIAL"
}

# Define headers
headers = {
    "Content-Type": "application/json",
    "X-Goog-Api-Key": "YOUR_API_KEY",
    "X-Goog-FieldMask": "routes.duration,routes.distanceMeters,routes.
    polyline.encodedPolyline"
}

# Make the request
response = requests.post("https://routes.googleapis.com/directions/
v2:computeRoutes", json=payload, headers=headers)

# Print the response
print(response.json())
```

> **Note**   In order for this code to run, you must set a date and time in the
> "DEPARTURE-TIME" parameter that is beyond the time at which you run the code.
> In other words, the departure time cannot be set in the past. In this example, the
> date is set to a specific time in 2025, but if you're running this code beyond that
> year, you need to adjust the code in the "DEPARTURE-TIME" parameter in order for
> your code to run as expected.

After running this code, this is the response you should get.

Listing 2-21. The Successful Response After Running the Code from ChatGPT

```
{'routes': [{'distanceMeters': 773, 'duration': '158s', 'polyline':
{'encodedPolyline': 'ipkcFjichVzQ@d@gU{E?'}}]}
```

Using ChatGPT to Avoid Reading a Lot of Documentation and Having to Decipher Through Any cURL Code

As mentioned before, there is a *lot* of documentation to go through in the Google Maps Platform. If you even took a cursory glance at the other APIs we passed by to get to the Routes API, in specific, you would have seen different APIs for pulling vast varieties of data; air quality, pollen, aerial view (like you'd see when you use Google Maps), and many other features of Google Maps you may normally take for granted all have individual APIs. Do you know what geocoding is? Well, you'd have to find out the hard way if you went through the documentation on your own.

Reading through documentation is annoying. Especially when we only want a few features in any given API or service. In a perfect world, we wouldn't even *need* to know what geocoding is in order to get our code working in different scenarios other than what's provided in the example code from Google.

We may not live in a perfect world, but we *don't* have to know what geocoding is, at least not anymore. We can simply use ChatGPT to get through the documentation we don't want to read.

Here's what we asked ChatGPT so you don't have to read any of the Google Maps Route API to get working code.

Listing 2-22. Prompting ChatGPT to Avoid Reading Documentation

I need to use the Google Maps Platform's Routes API gives me to pull down information pertaining to how much time it'll take to get from one destination to the other, as well as how much distance is between the two points. How can I make an HTTP request in Python to get the information I'm looking for?

This is the code we got in our response from ChatGPT.

Listing 2-23. Getting a Response Back from ChatGPT to Avoid Reading Documentation

```python
import requests

def get_route_info(google_maps_api_key, origin, destination):
    url = f"https://maps.googleapis.com/maps/api/directions/json?origin={or
        igin}&destination={destination}&key={google_maps_api_key}"
    response = requests.get(url)

    if response.status_code == 200:
        route_data = response.json()
        if route_data["status"] == "OK":
            route_info = route_data["routes"][0]["legs"][0]
            distance = route_info["distance"]["text"]
            duration = route_info["duration"]["text"]
            print(f"Distance: {distance}, Duration: {duration}")
        else:
            print("Error:", route_data["status"])
    else:
        print("Error:", response.status_code)
```

```
# Replace 'YOUR_GOOGLE_MAPS_API_KEY' with your actual Google Maps API key
google_maps_api_key = 'YOUR_GOOGLE_MAPS_API_KEY'
origin = 'New York, NY'  # Example origin
destination = 'Los Angeles, CA'  # Example destination

get_route_info(google_maps_api_key, origin, destination)
```

If you run this code, you should get this very clean, very simple response:

```
Distance: 2,789 mi, Duration: 1 day 17 hours
```

Conclusion

Let's debunk a common myth and set the record straight: ChatGPT isn't some mind-reading wizard! As an AI tool, it's not here to replace the expertise of developers and architects – it's here to complement it and save a lot of time and hassle in the day-to-day frustrations the average programmer faces on a regular bases. Sure, it can help translate your natural language requests into code, but let's not forget the crucial role of human judgment. Ultimately, it's up to developers to decide whether to use, tweak, or toss out the resulting code.

CHAPTER 3

Creating a Basic ChatGPT Client in Python

The purpose of this chapter is plain and simple. We're going to build the most powerful ChatGPT client available using only a few lines of code in python. This client will do a lot more than what you're able to do using the ChatGPT website and will provide you more options than what is available using the Chat Playground that we saw in Chapter 1.

Creating Our ChatGPT Chat Completion Application, chatgpt_client.py

Listing 3-1 is the code for our ChatGPT client, chatgpt_client.py.

Listing 3-1. chatgpt_client.py

```
"""
Script to demonstrate API call using OpenAI's GPT-4 for chat completions.
"""

from dotenv import load_dotenv
from openai import OpenAI

# Load environment variables from .env
load_dotenv()

#instantiate the OpenAI object
client = OpenAI()
```

© Lydia Evelyn, Bruce Hopkins 2024
L. Evelyn and B. Hopkins, *Beginning ChatGPT for Python*, https://doi.org/10.1007/979-8-8688-0929-3_3

```python
response = client.chat.completions.create(
    model="gpt-4o",
    messages=[
        {
            "role": "system",
            "content": "You are a Python developer"
        },
        {
            "role": "user",
            "content": "Why is Python typically used for data science?"
        }
    ],
    temperature=0.85,
    max_tokens=1921,
    top_p=1,
    frequency_penalty=0,
    presence_penalty=0
)

print(response)
```

As you analyze the code in Listing 3-1, you're going to see several things that are quite familiar from the Chat Playground such as the `model`, `messages`, `temperature`, and `tokens`.

Note   In this chapter, we'll use the Python datatypes, so you'll see a `list` where the official OpenAPI documentation specifies an `Array`.

Using **OpenAI.chat.completions.create()** to Send Messages to ChatGPT

The `OpenAI.chat.completions.create()` method is a method that's basically a one-to-one representation of what you can do in the Chat Playground; therefore, this method should feel like second nature to you.

Table 3-1 describes the format of the parameter necessary to call the OpenAI.chat. completions.create() method. Although the table is lengthy, after a quick glance, you should see that only a few fields are actually required in order to successfully invoke the method.

The response to the method is called a ChatCompletion.

Examining the Method Parameters

Table 3-1. *The Structure of the Create ChatCompletion Object*

Field	Type	Required?	Description
model	String	Required	The ID of the model you want to use for the ChatCompletion. Compatible models include • gpt-4 • gpt-4-0613 • gpt-4-32k • gpt-4-32k-0613 • gpt-4o • gpt-4o-mini • o1 • o1-mini
messages	List	Required	There are four types of messages, each with their own requirements: • System message (see Table 3-2) • User message (see Table 3-3) • Assistant message (see Table 3-4) • Tool message (see Table 3-5)

(continued)

Table 3-1. (*continued*)

Field	Type	Required?	Description
frequency_penalty	Number or null Default: 0	Optional	A number between -2.0 and 2.0. Positive values penalize tokens based on their existing frequency in the conversation history, reducing the likelihood of repeating the same lines verbatim.
logit_bias	JSON map Default: null	Optional	Allows you to modify the likelihood of specific tokens appearing in the completion. You provide a JSON object that maps tokens (specified by their token ID in the tokenizer) to associated bias values from -100 to 100. This bias is added to the model's logits before sampling.

(continued)

Table 3-1. (*continued*)

Field	Type	Required?	Description
logprobs	Boolean or null	Optional, defaults to false	This parameter enables you to decide if the log probabilities of the output tokens should be returned.
			When set to true, it provides the log probabilities for each output token included in the message content.
			However, this feature is presently not supported by the gpt-4-vision-preview model.
max_tokens	Integer or null	Optional	This parameter sets the maximum number of tokens that the generated ChatCompletion can have.
n	Integer or null Default: 1	Optional	Specifies how many ChatCompletion choices the model should generate for each input message.
presence_penalty	Number or null Default: 0	Optional	A number between -2.0 and 2.0. Positive values penalize new tokens based on whether they appear in the conversation history, encouraging the model to talk about new topics.

(*continued*)

Table 3-1. (*continued*)

Field	Type	Required?	Description
response_format	JSON object	Optional	You have two options: { "type": "json_object" } for a JSON object response or { "type": "text" } for a text response
			Note: It's crucial to remember that while operating in JSON mode, you need to explicitly command the model to generate JSON, either through a system or user directive.
			Failing to do so can cause the model to endlessly output whitespace until it hits the token cap, leading to a request that appears to be frozen.
			Additionally, be aware that if the finish_reason is "length," it suggests the generation went beyond the max tokens or the conversation exceeded the maximum allowable context length, which might result in the message being truncated.

(*continued*)

Table 3-1. (*continued*)

Field	Type	Required?	Description
seed	Integer or null	Optional	By specifying a seed, the system will make an attempt to generate repeatable results.
			In theory, this means that if you make repeated requests with the same seed and parameters, you should expect to receive the same result.
			In order to get the seed value to put in the subsequent request, copy the system_ fingerprint from your last response.
stop	String/list/ null Default: null	Optional	You can provide up to four sequences where the API should stop generating further tokens.
			This can be useful for controlling the length or content of responses.
stream	Boolean or null Default: false	Optional	If "stream" is set to "true," partial message updates will be sent as server-sent events.
			This means tokens will be sent as data-only events as they become available, and the stream will end with a "data: [DONE]" message.

(*continued*)

Table 3-1. (*continued*)

Field	Type	Required?	Description
temperature	Number or null	Optional	Valid values range between 0 and 2.
	Default: 1		Controls the randomness of the model's output.
			The best practice is to adjust the top_p or temperature, but not both.
tool_choice	String or JSON object	Optional	This parameter controls which (if any) function is called by the model. You have two options: "none" or "auto."
			Use "none" if you don'''''t want the model to call a function.
			Use "auto" if you want the model to pick between generating a message or calling a function.
			Specifying a particular function via {"type": "function", "function": {"name": "my_function"}} forces the model to call that function.
			Please note that "none" is the default when no functions are present and "auto" is the default if functions are present.

(*continued*)

Table 3-1. (*continued*)

Field	Type	Required?	Description
tools	List	Optional	Optionally, you can specify a list of tools the model may call.
			Currently, only functions are supported as a tool.
			Use this to provide a list of functions the model may generate JSON inputs for.
top_logprobs	Integer or null	Optional	This can be any integer from 0 to 5.
			It's used to determine the count of the most probable tokens to return at each token position, accompanied by their respective log probabilities.
			For this parameter to be applicable, logprobs must be enabled by setting it to true.
top_p	Number or null	Optional	Valid values range between 0 and 1.
	Default: 1		Indicates whether to consider few possibilities (0) or all possibilities (1).
			The best practice is to adjust the top_p or temperature, but not both.
user	String	Optional	This is a unique ID that you can optionally generate to represent your end-user.
			This will help OpenAI monitor and detect abuse.

OK, Table 3-1 appears to be a little daunting! However, as mentioned earlier, only the model and messages are required parameters.

Additionally, we also have the code in Listing 3-1 above in order to show how the parameters are actually used within a real application.

So, as you can see, as a Python developer, we have several options and parameters available to use that ordinary people can't do using the ChatGPT website or using the Chat Playground.

Now, the one parameter that needs the most detailed explanation is the messages parameter, so let's analyze that further.

There Are Four Types of Messages

When invoking the ChatGPT API programmatically, there are four types of messages that you can provide to the API:

- System message
- User message
- Assistant message
- Tool message

The good news is that if you refer back to Chapter 1 where we explained how to use the Chat Playground, you can see that we've already have encountered the first three message types! The only new message type that we're not currently familiar with is the tool message."

System Message (Dictionary)

Table 3-2. *The Structure of the System Message*

Field	Type	Required?	Description
role	String	Required	This must be set to the string, "system"
content	String	Required	These are the instructions that you want the system to perform in the conversation.
name	String	Optional	This is an optional name that you can provide the system.

Listing 3-2 is a snippet from Listing 3-1 that shows how the system message is formatted.

Listing 3-2. Formatting the System Message

```
messages=[
    {
        "role": "system",
        "content": "You are a Python developer"
    },
    ...
```

User Message (Dictionary)

Table 3-3. *The Structure of the User Message*

Field	Type	Required?	Description
role	String	Required	This must be set to the string, "user"
content	String	Required	This string contains the actual message or question that you want to send to ChatGPT.
name	String	Optional	This is an optional name that you can provide for yourself in the conversation.

Listing 3-3 is a snippet from Listing 3-1 that shows how the user message is formatted.

Listing 3-3. Formatting the User Message

```
messages=[
    ...
    {
        "role": "user",
        "content": "Why is Python typically used for data science?"
    }
    ...
```

Assistant Message (Dictionary)

Note   In case you forgot, the assistant message is used to "remind" ChatGPT what it told you in a previous response. Ideally, this can allow you to continue a conversation that you had with it weeks or months in the past.

Table 3-4. *The Structure of the Assistant Message*

Field	Type	Required?	Description
role	String	Required	This must be set to the string, "assistant"
content	String	Required	This string contains the response from ChatGPT from a previous conversation.
name	String	Optional	This is an optional name that you can provide for ChatGPT in the conversation.
tool_calls	List	Optional	If ChatGPT used a tool in a previous response, then include the tool that it specified here.
↳ id	String	Required	This is the ID of the tool called by ChatGPT.
↳ type	String	Required	This is the type of the tool called by ChatGPT. Only the literal, "function," is a valid tool.
↳ function	Object	Required	This is the function that the model called.

Listing 3-4 is a snippet from Listing 3-1 that shows how the assistant message is formatted.

Listing 3-4. Formatting the Assistant Message

```
messages=[
    ...
        {
            "role": "assistant",
```

```
    "content": "Python is typically used for data science for
    several reasons..."
  }
...
```

Tool Message (Dictionary)

A tool message is an advanced type of message for a very specific use case. You can't use them on the ChatGPT website nor in the Chat Playground. Using a tool message and the tool parameter from Table 3-1, you can enable ChatGPT to "call a function" for you.

At first glance, you may be thinking, "Wow! ChatGPT will load my code and execute it for me in the Cloud? That's awesome!" Unfortunately, that's not the case.

By providing a function name and the parameters necessary to invoke it, ChatGPT will let you know whether to invoke the function and the parameters to put in the function. You will then need to call the function *yourself* within your Python code.

Table 3-5. *The Structure of the Tool Message*

Field	Type	Required?	Description
role	String	Required	This must be set to the string, "tool"
content	String	Required	This string contains the content of the tool message.
tool_call_id	List	Optional	This is the ID of the tool call.

Running `chatgpt_client.py`

So, after running the code we created in Listing 3-1, we can expect a response that will look something like this in Listing 3-5.

Listing 3-5. ChatGPT Explains Why Python Is So Awesome

```
ChatCompletion(id='chatcmpl-9ACnRg1bk54jYeIFbxJ3yDnomQmij',
choices=[Choice(finish_reason='stop', index=0, message=ChatCompletion
```

Message(content="Python is typically used for data science for several reasons:\n\n1. **Simplicity and Readability**: Python's syntax is clear and straightforward, which makes the code easy to read and write. This simplicity allows data scientists to quickly understand Python's syntax and start coding faster.\n\n2. **Versatile Library Ecosystem**: Python has a wide range of libraries and tools designed specifically for data science tasks. Libraries like NumPy and SciPy are great for scientific computation, Pandas is excellent for data manipulation and analysis, Matplotlib and Seaborn for data visualization, and libraries like Scikit-learn for machine learning.\n\n3. **Support for Different Data Formats**: Python supports a variety of data formats which are commonly used in data science. You can easily load and handle data in different formats such as CSV, Excel spreadsheets, SQL databases, and more.\n\n4. **Community Support**: Python has a large and active community of developers who constantly contribute to improving the language and its tools. This also means that when problems arise, it's usually easier to find solutions and examples in Python than in less popular languages.\n\n5. **Integration Capability**: Python can easily integrate with other languages like C, C++, Java, and it can also be run on almost all operating systems. This makes it a convenient choice for data scientists who need to work with different software and systems.\n\n6. **Support for Advanced Data Analysis**: Python supports various types of advanced data analysis, including machine learning, artificial intelligence, and deep learning, with libraries like TensorFlow, PyTorch, and Keras. \n\n7. **Ideal for Prototyping**: Python's simplicity and speed make it ideal for prototyping. Data scientists can use Python to build a model, see how it works, and then use Python or another language to build a more permanent version if necessary.", role='assistant', function_call=None, tool_calls=None), logprobs=None)], created=1712219497, model='gpt-4-0613', object='chat.completion', system_fingerprint=None, usage=CompletionUsage(completion_tokens=368, prompt_tokens=25, total_tokens=393))

So, as we take a brief look at Listing 3-5, we see that a bulk of the response (called a ChatCompletion) is the answer to our question that we posed to ChatGPT in Listing 3-1 at the very beginning of the chapter. However, there's a lot of metadata around our response, and let's analyze the ChatCompletion object in more detail.

Handling the Response (ChatCompletion)

Table 3-6. *The Structure of the ChatCompletion Object Response*

Field	Type	Description
id	String	A distinct identifier for the ChatCompletion.
choices	List	A list of ChatCompletion options. There can be multiple options in the response if "n" is greater than 1 in Table 3-1.
⌐ finish_reason	String	Every response will include a finish_reason. The possible values for finish_reason are
		stop: The API returned complete message or a message terminated by one of the stop sequences provided via the stop parameter.
		length: The model output was incomplete due to the max_tokens parameter in the request or token limit of the model itself.
		tool_call: The model called a tool, such as a function.
		content_filter: The response was terminated due to a violation of the content filters.
		null: The API response still in progress or incomplete.
⌐ index	Integer	The index of the choice in the list of choices.
⌐ message	Object	A ChatCompletionMessage generated by the model. This is explained in further detail in Table 3-7.
⌐ logprobs	Object or null	Log probability information for the choice.
model	String	The model used for the ChatCompletion.
system_fingerprint	String	Use this parameter as the "seed" in a subsequent request if you want to reproducible results in from a previous conversation.
object	String	This always returns the literal, "chat.completion."

(continued)

71

Table 3-6. (*continued*)

Field	Type	Description
usage	Object	Usage statistics for the completion request.
↳ completion_tokens	Integer	Number of tokens in the generated completion.
↳ prompt_tokens	Integer	Number of tokens in the prompt.
↳ total_tokens	Integer	The total count of tokens utilized in the request, including both the prompt and the completion.

The most important item in the ChatCompletion object is the ChatCompletionMessage which is explained in more detail in Table 3-7.

ChatCompletionMessage

Table 3-7. *The Structure of the ChatCompletionMessage*

Field	Type	Description
role	String	This will always be the literal, "assistant."
content	String or null	This is a string that contains the response from ChatGPT to our request.
tool_calls	List	If you indicated in Table 3-1 that you want ChatGPT to call a tool (which is currently a function), then this list will exist in the ChatCompletionMessage.
↳ id	String	This is the ID of the tool called by ChatGPT.
↳ type	String	This is the type of the tool called by ChatGPT. Only the literal, "function," is a valid tool.
↳ function	Object	This is the function and the parameters that the model called.

Conclusion

In this chapter, we took our experiences from Chapters 1 and 2 and created a fully functioning ChatGPT client in Python. In the code for our ChatGPT client, we saw some terms that we were already introduced to from the Chat Playground such as the `model`, `messages`, `temperature`, and `tokens`.

We also saw that, as Python developers, OpenAI gives us a **ton of additional options** to invoke ChatGPT that aren't available to average everyday users or even to technical people who use the Chat Playground. In this chapter, we took the time to explain these options, with a focus on the `messages` that we can send.

Now that we have a working ChatGPT client in Python, let's see how to leverage it for the rest of the examples in the book!

CHAPTER 4

Using AI in the Enterprise! Creating a Text Summarizer for Slack Messages

In today's corporate world, it's extremely common for companies to have an instance of Slack (or Microsoft Teams) to organize themselves and use it as a central place of communication to everyone in the company. Now, if you've ever used Slack before, I think you know how easily a channel can become flooded with a ton of messages because **some** important thing happened **somewhere** in the company or the world.

Of course, the more responsibility that you have within the company (i.e., manager, team leader, architect, etc.), the more channels you're expected to participate in. In my opinion, Slack is a double-edged sword. You need to use it to do your job, but as a developer, you definitely can't attend a daily standup meeting and say, "Yesterday, uh, I spent all day reading Slack. No roadblocks."

Additionally, if you work for a company with clients in various time zones (which is quite common nowadays), it's pretty daunting to open Slack in the morning and see a ton of messages that were posted while you were away from the keyboard.

So, in this chapter, we're going to apply AI in the enterprise to make Slack more useful. We'll leverage the code in the previous chapter and create a Slack bot in Python that will summarize the important conversations in a Slack channel. We're going to be utilizing ChatGPT's capabilities for text summarization and focus a bit more on **prompt engineering**.

© Lydia Evelyn, Bruce Hopkins 2024
L. Evelyn and B. Hopkins, *Beginning ChatGPT for Python*, https://doi.org/10.1007/979-8-8688-0929-3_4

So, What Is Prompt Engineering?

Simply stated, prompt engineering is the process of carefully crafting and refining prompts and input parameters to instruct and guide the behavior of ChatGPT and other AI models. It's basically the industry-wide term for creating the right input in order to get the result that you're looking for.

ChatGPT Is Here to Take Away Everyone's Jobs (Not Really)

It is my humble opinion that every company in the world is sitting on a gold mine of untapped information. If you are using any system that keeps a log of exchanges between employees, a database of support requests from your customers, or any large repository of text (yes this includes your email, Microsoft Exchange, and corporate Gmail), then, you have a large repository of unstructured text that is waiting to be utilized.

Therefore, the best use of ChatGPT is not to eliminate anyone's jobs. It should be used in order to augment and extend what team members in your company are already doing. As we saw in the previous chapter, as a programmer, ChatGPT can work as a very effective pair-programmer. It is also very good at performing certain difficult tasks very efficiently and quickly. Therefore, the project of this chapter involves tackling a practical example of what can be done in order to make useful a large source of unstructured text.

You can use the ChatGPT client you created in Chapter 3 for the prompt engineering examples listed further on in this chapter, or you can use the playground mode feature we talked about in Chapter 1. Either way, let's dive right in.

Examining a Real-World Problem: Customer Support for a Software Company

Let's look at one of the most grueling tasks in software development: providing tech support. Imagine the joys of fielding calls and messages all day from people who might be frustrated, confused, or just in need of a solution while using your software. Here's some of the reasons why customer support is a tough nut to crack:

- Your end-users and your customers are notoriously bad at explaining problems with your software.

- Level 1 technicians, often the first line of defense, typically handle the most basic issues or user errors. But when problems get more complex, users are escalated to Level 2.

- The mid-tier is a tricky place, because they have more knowledge and experience than the tech support staff at Level 1; however, they don't have the opportunity to directly get answers from the end-user.

- Really bad problems get escalated to Level 3; however, these are the most expensive tech support staff because they have the most knowledge and experience. They have hands-on experience with the code as well as the servers and the infrastructure.

So, let's work with a real-world example of a typical conversation within a typical tech support channel within Slack. Below is a list of the team members and their roles within a fictional company:

- Fatima (customer service representative)

- John (software engineer)

- Dave (PM)

- Keith (CTO)

The listing below provides an example of a conversation between the team members at a software startup. Fatima, the customer service representative, lets the team know that their app is crashing immediately after launching (not a good problem to have). Keith, the CTO, steps in immediately to escalate the issue.

Listing 4-1. Team Members Within a Slack Channel Trying to Analyze a Customer's Problem

Fatima [16:00 | 02/08/2019]: Hey everyone, I have an urgent issue to discuss. I just got off a call with a client who's experiencing app crashes as soon as they load it. They're really frustrated. Can we get this sorted ASAP? ☹

Keith [16:01 | 02/08/2019]: Thanks for bringing this to our attention, Fatima. Let's jump on this right away. @John, can you take the lead in investigating the issue since our architect is out sick today?

John [16:02 | 02/08/2019]: Sure thing, Keith. I'll dive into the codebase and see if I can find any potential culprits for the crashes.

John [16:02 | 02/08/2019]: Fatima, could you gather some additional information from the client? Ask them about the specific device, operating system, and any recent updates they might have installed.

Fatima [16:03 | 02/08/2019]: Absolutely, John. I'll reach out to the client immediately and gather those details. Will update you all once I have them.

Dave [16:04 | 02/08/2019]: I understand the urgency here. Let's make sure we keep the client informed about our progress 💯 Fatima. We don't want them feeling left in the dark during this troubleshooting process.

Fatima [16:04 | 02/08/2019]: Definitely, Dave. 👍 I'll keep the client updated at regular intervals, providing them with any relevant information we uncover.

John [16:20 | 02/08/2019]: I've checked the codebase, and so far, I haven't found any obvious issues. It's strange that the app is crashing on load. Could it be a memory-related issue? Keith, do we have any recent reports of memory leaks or high memory usage?

Keith [16:22 | 02/08/2019]: I'll pull up the monitoring logs, John, and check if there have been any memory-related anomalies in recent releases. Let me get back to you on that.

Fatima [17:01 | 02/08/2019]: Quick update, everyone. The client is using an iPhone X running iOS 15.1. They mentioned that the issue started after updating their app a few days ago 😩

Keith [17:05 | 02/08/2019]: Thanks for the update, Fatima. That's helpful information. John, let's focus on testing the latest app update on an iPhone X simulator with iOS 15.1 to see if we can replicate the issue.

John [17:06 | 02/08/2019]: Good idea, Keith. I'll set up the emulator and run some tests right away.

Keith [17:30 | 02/08/2019]: John, any progress on replicating the issue on the emulator?

John [17:32 | 02/08/2019]: Yes, Keith. I managed to reproduce the crash on the emulator. It seems to be related to a compatibility issue with iOS 15.1 😵. I suspect it's due to a deprecated method call. I'll fix it and run more tests to confirm.

John [18:03 | 02/08/2019]: Fixed the deprecated method issue, and the app is no longer crashing on load. It looks like we've identified and resolved the problem. I'll prepare a patch and send it to you, Keith, for review and deployment.

Keith [18:04 | 02/08/2019]: 🙌🙌🙌 Thank you, please provide me with the patch as soon as possible. Once I review it, we'll deploy the fix to the app store.

Dave [18:06 | 02/08/2019]: Great job, team! 🎉 John, please keep the client informed about the progress and let them know we have a fix ready for them on the next app update. Can someone make sure the release notes reflect this?

John [18:07 | 02/08/2019]: Will do, Dave. I'll update the client and ensure they're aware of the upcoming fix.

Keith [18:27 | 02/08/2019]: Patch reviewed and approved, John. Please proceed with updating the app in the store. Let's aim to have it done within the next hour.

John [18:26 | 02/08/2019]: Understood, Keith. I'm in the process of uploading it now.

Fatima [18:38 | 02/08/2019]: I just informed the client about the fix. They're relieved and grateful for our prompt response. Thanks, everyone, for your collaboration and quick action. It's a pleasure working with such a competent team!

Dave [18:40 | 02/08/2019]: Well done, team! Your efforts are greatly appreciated. We managed to turn this urgent problem around in record time. Let's keep up the good work! 👍

Prompt Engineering 101: Text Summarization

So, needless to say, no one wants to spend their day constantly scrolling through Slack channels reading about issues and problems that are on fire. We're going to utilize the capabilities of ChatGPT for text summarization. To keep things simple, let's try a few prompts to send the entire listing of the chat messages to ChatGPT in order for it to give us a usable summary of all the events that have happened.

Prompt #1: "tl;dr"

This prompt is short, sweet, and to the point. In case you're not familiar with it, it's a term used online frequently to briefly summarize a long article. It literally stands for "too long; didn't read," which is how I feel about a lot of conversations on Slack when I'm swamped with work. Conveniently, ChatGPT can understand this simple term (I wouldn't necessarily call it a word) as a prompt, and the results are pretty impressive.

Listing 4-2. PROMPT. Asking for a Summarized Version of a Longer Conversation

```
System: You are a helpful assistant
User:   Fatima [16:00 | 02/08/2019]: Hey everyone, I have an urgent ...
User:   Tl;dr
Model: gpt-4o
Temperature: 1
Maximum length: 360
Top P: 1
Frequency penalty: 0
Presence penalty: 0
```

Notice how the number of tokens is kept small, at 360, which will ultimately help ChatGPT to create a short response. Also, see that the temperature is left at 1 (the default value), but the Top P is increased all the way to its maximum (which is 1). Therefore, it's important to play around with temperature and other settings to control the tone and variety of ChatGPT's responses.

Listing 4-3 below shows ChatGPT's summarization of the conversation from Listing 4-1.

Listing 4-3. RESPONSE. Getting a Summarized Version of a Very Long Conversation

The team quickly responds to a client's app crashing issue. John investigates the codebase while Fatima gathers information from the client. They discover a compatibility issue with iOS 15.1 and John fixes it. The patch is reviewed and approved, and the app is updated in the store. The client is informed and grateful for the quick resolution. The team is praised for their collaboration and prompt action.

That's fantastic! It reduced that extremely long conversation down to a simple and brief summary of only 68 words. As you can see, ChatGPT is not replacing a job here; however, it will definitely make someone more productive. Now, let's try a few more prompts, shall we?

Prompt #2: "Explain This in Three Sentences or Less"

So, If "tl;dr" doesn't provide a brief enough explanation for you, then we can tell ChatGPT to make things even simpler. ChatGPT does well with parameters, so let's specify that the explanation shouldn't be any longer than three sentences.

Listing 4-4. PROMPT. Asking for a Shorter Version of a Longer Conversation

System: You are a helpful assistant
User: Fatima [16:00 | 02/08/2019]: Hey everyone, I have an urgent ...
User: Explain this in 3 sentences or less.
Model: gpt-4o
Temperature: 1
Maximum length: 250

Top P: 0
Frequency penalty: 0
Presence penalty: 0

As you may have noticed, the temperature is set to 0.82 in this example. We really want ChatGPT to give us a concise answer here, so the "drier," the better.

Listing 4-5. RESPONSE. Getting a Three-Sentence Summary

```
A customer reported an urgent issue of app crashes to the team. John
investigates the issue and asks Fatima to gather additional information
from the client. They discover that the issue is related to a compatibility
problem with iOS 15.1. John fixes the problem and Keith approves the
deployment of the fix to the client's production environment.
```

Prompt #3: "I'm a Manager. Explain to Me What Happened"

When you don't want to sound like the one person that doesn't understand, ChatGPT has the capability to rephrase what has been said and break it down until it's very simple.

Listing 4-6. PROMPT. Asking for a Simplified Version of a More Complex Conversation

```
System: You are a helpful assistant
User:   Fatima [16:00 | 02/08/2019]: Hey everyone, I have an urgent ...
User: Summarize this conversation and explain it to me like I'm a manager
with little technical experience.
Model: gpt-4o
Temperature: 0.82
Maximum length: 750
Top P: 1
Frequency penalty: 0
Presence penalty: 0
```

Again, the temperature is set below 1.0 so that ChatGPT can keep the answer brief and easy to understand. We increased the token length so that ChatGPT can take the time to explain some potentially technical concepts.

Listing 4-7. RESPONSE. Getting a Simplified Version of a More Complex Conversation

In this conversation, Fatima brings up an urgent issue with a client who is experiencing app crashes as soon as they load it. Keith assigns John to investigate the issue since their architect is out sick. John asks Fatima to gather additional information from the client about their device, operating system, and recent updates. Dave emphasizes the importance of keeping the client informed throughout the troubleshooting process.

John checks the codebase but doesn't find any obvious issues, so he suspects it could be a memory-related problem. Keith agrees to check for memory-related anomalies in recent releases. Fatima provides an update that the client is using an iPhone X running iOS 15.1 and mentioned that the issue started after updating the app. Keith suggests testing the latest app update on an iPhone X simulator with iOS 15.1 to replicate the issue.

John successfully reproduces the crash on the emulator and identifies a compatibility issue with iOS 15.1, possibly due to a deprecated method call. He fixes the issue and prepares a patch for review and deployment. Keith approves the patch and asks John to update the app in the store. Dave requests that the client be kept informed and that the release notes reflect the upcoming fix.

John uploads the patch and informs the client about the fix. Keith reviews and approves the patch, and John proceeds with updating the app in the store. Fatima informs the client about the fix, and they express relief and gratitude for the prompt response. Dave commends the team for their collaboration and quick action, emphasizing the importance of maintaining good work.

In summary, the team quickly addressed an urgent issue where a client's app was crashing on load. They investigated the issue, identified a compatibility problem with iOS 15.1, fixed it, and prepared a patch for deployment. The client was kept informed throughout the process, and the fix was successfully implemented, resulting in a relieved and grateful client.

Prompt #4: "Give Me Suggestions on Next Steps"

In addition to making a summary that's easier to understand, ChatGPT can explain in different styles and "tones." We're going to increase the Top P to 0.75 because we want ChatGPT to think of more possibilities than what is the default. We are also going to increase the presence penalty to 0.5 because we want to encourage a versatile response.

Listing 4-8. PROMPT. Asking to ChatGPT for Advice on the Best Next Steps

System: You are a helpful assistant
User: Fatima [16:00 | 02/08/2019]: Hey everyone, I have an urgent ...
User: I'm a QA engineer at the company. Give me suggestions on next steps.
Model: gpt-4o
Temperature: 1
Maximum length: 1200
Top P: 0.75
Frequency penalty: 0
Presence penalty: 0.5

Listing 4-9. RESPONSE. Suggestions from ChatGPT on Possible Next Steps

As a QA engineer, here are some suggestions for next steps:

1. Test the patch: Once the patch has been deployed to the app store, thoroughly test it on various devices and operating systems to ensure that the issue has been resolved and there are no new bugs or regressions introduced.

2. Conduct regression testing: In addition to testing the specific issue, perform a comprehensive regression test to ensure that the fix does not have any unintended side effects on other functionalities of the app.

3. Communicate the fix to the client: Keep the client updated on the progress and let them know that the fix is available in the latest app update. Provide them with clear instructions on how to update their app and encourage them to test it on their end as well.

4. Monitor user feedback: Keep an eye on user feedback after the fix has been deployed. Encourage users to report any issues they encounter, and be proactive in addressing them promptly.

5. Document the issue and resolution: Create a detailed report documenting the issue, the steps taken to reproduce and resolve it, and any other relevant information. This will serve as a reference for future troubleshooting and help improve the development process.

6. Conduct a post-mortem analysis: After the issue has been resolved and the fix has been deployed, schedule a post-mortem meeting with the team to discuss the root cause, lessons learned, and any process improvements that can be implemented to prevent similar issues in the future.

7. Continuous improvement: Use this incident as an opportunity to identify areas of improvement in the development and testing processes. Evaluate if there are any changes that can be made to prevent similar issues from occurring in the future.

Remember, open communication, collaboration, and continuous learning are key to ensuring the highest quality of your app and maintaining a strong relationship with your clients.

Now, of course, ChatGPT (like every other form of artificial intelligence on the planet) is not entirely perfect. For instance, recommendation number three is a valid item to do, except for the fact that it's not usually the responsibility of a QA person to communicate anything directly to the client or customer. That communication can be done either through tech support or with a product manager who has those communication channels (especially if they are a significant customer). So, the suggestion is fine, but it's not appropriate for a person with that role within a company.

Let's Talk About Real Prompt Engineering

If you Google the term "prompt engineering," you'll find a ton of examples, blogs, and even full websites with subscription plans that will try to convince you that the perfect prompts can be created by simply only using text. As you have seen from the examples above, prompt engineering cannot be accomplished solely by merely crafting textual inputs.

In reality, the process is quite similar to cooking a sophisticated meal. Imagine trying to cook, for example, beef bourguignon using only salt as the seasoning and neglecting all other ingredients and spices! Honestly, the result would pale in comparison to the actual dish.

Similarly, try assembling an entire orchestra but only use one instrument and one musician. That's an embarrassing "one-man band." Therefore, simply adjusting the text to the prompt isn't enough in order to truly perform prompt engineering. The parameters such as the model's temperature, which controls randomness; the Top P, impacting token probability; the specific model used; the number of tokens; and the other parameters all play highly pivotal roles in getting a great response.

This book is not about prompt engineering, since (as you can see from the explanation above) it truly involves several factors that don't have anything to do with Python. However, you are highly encouraged to experiment with *all* the parameters to the models provided by OpenAI to find what works best for your use case.

Registering a Slack Bot App

Now that we know the various ways for ChatGPT to summarize a large body of text for us, let's see what's necessary in order to create a simple bot in Python that will programmatically grab all the messages from a channel within a Slack instance.

Note   In order to accomplish these steps, you will need to have administrative access to a Slack workspace. Most developers will **not** have these levels of permissions; therefore, in order to fully experiment, I recommend that you create your own personal Slack workspace for testing purposes. This way, you will have all the rights and privileges to install your Slack bot.

But, one step at a time. First, we're going to make our Slack bot app, so head over the Slack API website:

```
https://api.slack.com/
```

Figure 4-1. *In Order to Create a Slack Bot, Go To the Slack API Website*

Of course, you'll need to have a Slack account in order for this to work, so if you don't have one, then you need to create one first.

After you have logged in, go to the top-right of the page and navigate to "Your apps > Create your first app," as shown in Figure 4-1 above. In Slack terminology, a "bot" is an "app," and bots are not allowed to run on a Slack instance unless they have been registered with Slack first.

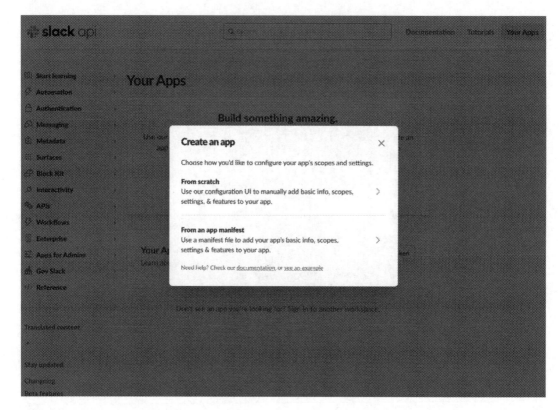

Figure 4-2. *Creating a New Bot App for Slack*

As shown in Figure 4-2, above, you'll be taken to the **Your Apps** page where you can manage your Slack apps. Immediately, you'll see a pop-up to **Create an App** button in the middle of the screen.

Select the option to create your app **from scratch**. This is because we want to be able to manipulate all of the details of the application ourselves without overcomplicating things with a bunch of default settings.

Afterwards, you'll be prompted to specify a name for your bot and to select the workspace that you want your bot to have access to, as shown in Figure 4-3 below.

Click the **Create App** button to proceed.

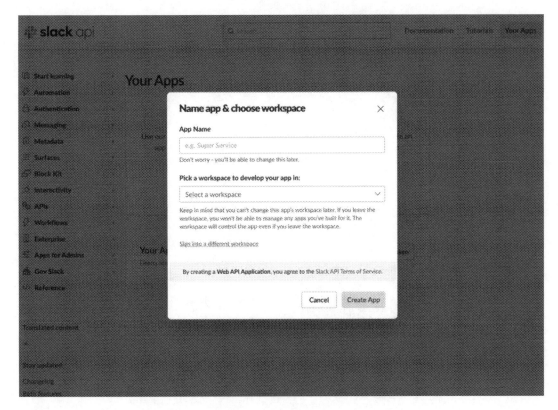

Figure 4-3. *Creating a New Bot App for Slack*

Specifying What Your Bot Can (and Can't) Do by Setting the Scope

Now, you'll be presented with a screen that has a ton of options for bots for Slack workspaces. The first thing you need to do, however, is from the sidebar on the left, click **OAuth & Permissions**.

Our bot is going to be pretty simple; all it needs to do is read the messages from a channel in order to give us a summary of what was said. In addition to reading the messages, we also need to know the names of the people in the Slack workspace, otherwise, we'll get a UUID representation of the person instead of their name, which is meaningless to us.

So, scroll down to add the following OAuth Scope to your Slack bot, as shown in Figure 4-4, below.

- channels:history

- channels:read

- users:read

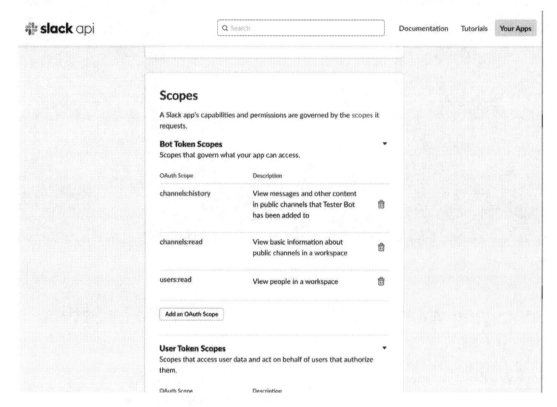

Figure 4-4. *Adding Scopes for the Slack Bot App*

Confirming Your Settings

After you've added the appropriate scopes for your bot, scroll back up and click on **Basic Information** from the left side bar.

On the page that follows, you'll see that there's now a green checkmark beside "Add features and functionality," which confirms that you've added your scopes correctly, as shown in Figure 4-5.

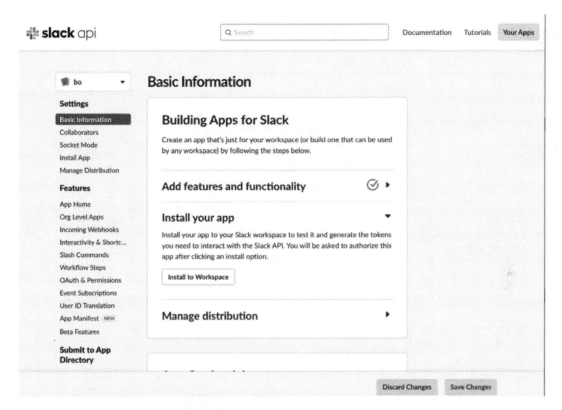

Figure 4-5. *Confirm Your Settings*

Viewing the OAuth & Permissions Page

As shown in Figure 4-6, below, navigate to the **OAuth & Permissions** page, and click on the "Install to Workspace" button.

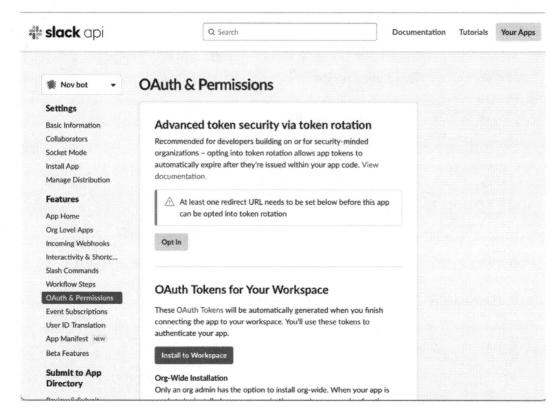

Figure 4-6. *The OAuth & Permissions Screen*

Installing Your Slack Bot App to Your Workspace

Now that all the permissions have been requested, it's time to install your bot to your workspace. During the installation process, you should see a screen as shown in Figure 4-7 below.

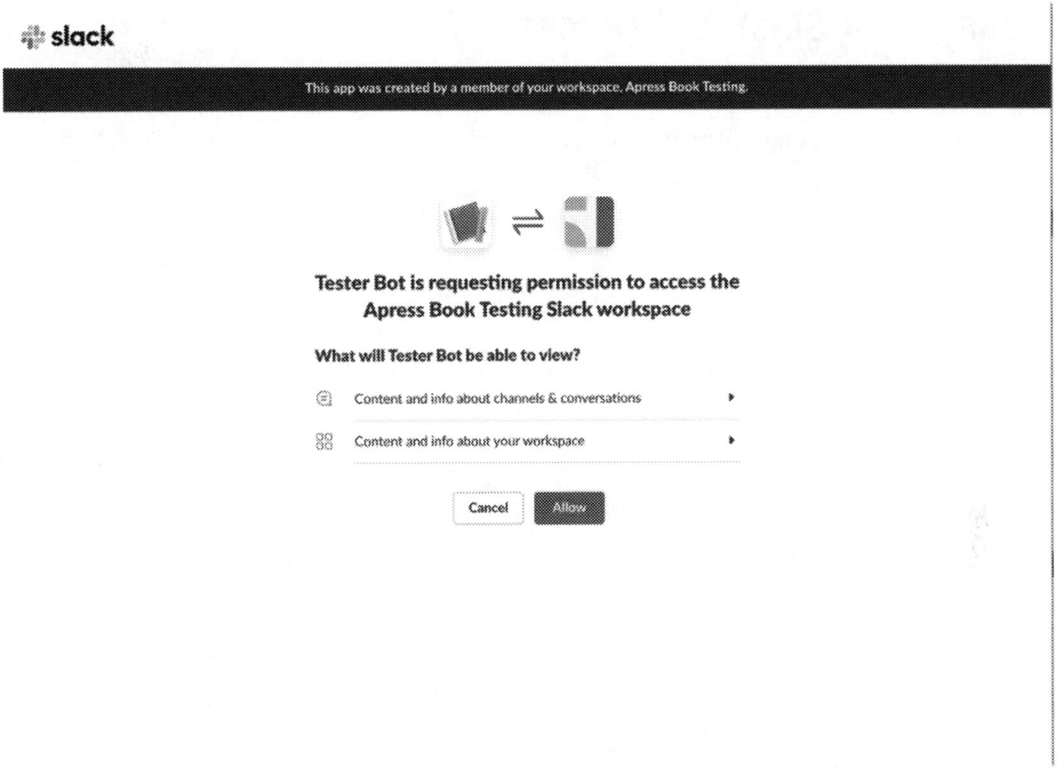

Figure 4-7. *"Installing" a New Slack Bot App*

Click the **Allow** button to authorize the bot and allow the permissions you allotted in the previous step.

Note   It's important to understand what "installing" means here. In a traditional Python sense, installing an app means to copy your files and dependencies to another machine and have it execute. That's not what's happening here.

Here, when you "install" a bot app, you're enabling your Slack workspace to allow an app to join the workspace – that's all. The code for your bot will run on your own machine and not on Slack's servers.

Getting Your Slack Bot (Access) Token

This time, "token" actually means access token! In order to connect to the Slack API and access messages and user information programmatically, you need a specific OAuth token generated for your Slack bot.

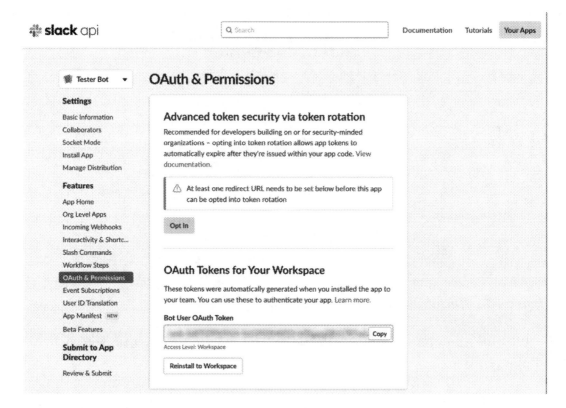

Figure 4-8. *Copy Your OAuth Token for Your Slack Bot App*

Back on the **OAuth & Permissions** page, be sure to copy the bot token (which usually starts with "xoxb-") from the page here, as shown in Figure 4-8.

Inviting Your Bot to Your Channel

Next, you're going to go to the channel you'd like to use to test your bot and type in the following command in the channel itself.

```
/invite
```

Select the option "Add apps to this channel," and then select the name of the Slack bot that you specified earlier when you registered the bot with Slack.

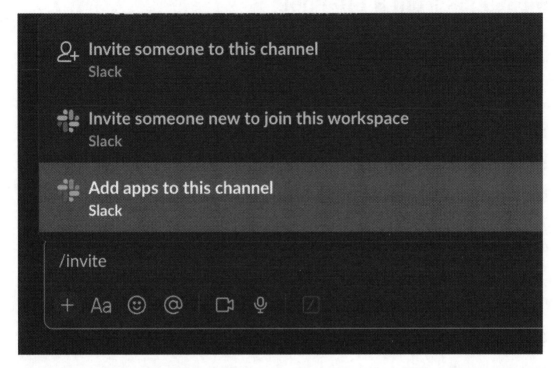

Figure 4-9. *Adding Your Slack Bot to a Channel*

Congratulations! You now have successfully registered a Slack bot app with Slack, enabled it to read messages in your workspace, and added the Slack bot to a channel. Before we can write the Python code to access the channel in our workspace, we need to know what is the internal ID that Slack uses for our channel.

Finding the Channel ID of Your Channel

Ok, this is an easy step to do. In Slack, right-click on the name of your channel and select the option "View Channel details." At the bottom of the pop-up window is the ID of your channel. Copy that number and save it for later. Your Python app will need this in order to join the right channel in your Slack workspace.

Using Your Slack Bot App to Automatically Grab Messages from a Channel

Alright, now that we have done all the prerequisites and we know the ID of our channel, let's get to the code in Python that accesses all the messages from a particular Slack channel.

Programmatically Reading Messages from Slack with **slack_chat_reader_bot.py**

First things first, you need to install the official Python Slack library, slack_sdk. You can use pip install like this:

pip install slack_sdk

Listing 4-10 is a simple Python Slack bot that obtains the user name, timestamp, and message content of each posting in the channel within a designated time period.

Listing 4-10. slack_chat_reader_bot.py

```
from slack_sdk import WebClient
from slack_sdk.errors import SlackApiError
from datetime import datetime, timezone

# Define your Slack API token
SLACK_BOT_TOKEN = "YOUR_SLACK_API_TOKEN"

# Initialize a WebClient instance
client = WebClient(token=SLACK_BOT_TOKEN)

# Define your channel ID
channel_id = "YOUR_CHANNEL_ID"

# Define start and end time in UTC
start_time_utc = datetime(2024, 8, 3, 10, 0, tzinfo=timezone.utc)
end_time_utc = datetime(2024, 8, 12, 15, 0, tzinfo=timezone.utc)
```

```python
# Convert start and end time to Unix timestamps
start_time_unix = int(start_time_utc.timestamp())
end_time_unix = int(end_time_utc.timestamp())

try:
    # Call the conversations.history method using WebClient
    response = client.conversations_history(
        channel=channel_id,
        oldest=start_time_unix,
        latest=end_time_unix,
    )

    # Check if the API call was successful
    if response["ok"]:
        # Reverse the messages list to get them in chronological order
        messages = reversed(response["messages"])
        for message in messages:
            user_id = message.get("user")
            timestamp = datetime.fromtimestamp(float(message.get("ts")),
            tz=timezone.utc)
            user_info_response = client.users_info(user=user_id)
            if user_info_response["ok"]:
                user_name = user_info_response["user"]["name"]
                print("User:", user_name)
                print("Timestamp:", timestamp)
                print("Message:", message.get("text"))
                print()
            else:
                print("Failed to fetch user info:", user_info_
                response["error"])
    else:
        print("Failed to fetch messages:", response["error"])
except SlackApiError as e:
    print(f"Error: {e.response['error']}")
```

Let's walk through this code together. First, we're importing essential modules for interfacing with the Slack API and managing date/time data. We then define the Slack API token (SLACK_BOT_TOKEN) needed for authentication, along with the ID of the target Slack channel (channel_id).

Next, we establish the start and end times for the message retrieval window, specifying them in coordinated universal time (UTC). Our script converts these time values into Unix timestamps since the Slack API expects timestamps in this format for message retrieval.

If the API call is successful, our script proceeds to extract and process the messages. Messages are presented in chronological order so that the oldest messages appear first. To keep things clean, for each message, the script retrieves the user ID and message timestamp. It then uses the `client.users_info` method to fetch additional information about the user who sent the message.

In case of any errors during the API request process (SlackApiError), the script catches and handles them by printing an error message.

Listing 4-11 shows the output after executing `slack_chat_reader_bot.py`, which is truncated here since you already have the full text in Listing 4-1 earlier in this chapter.

Listing 4-11. The Output from Executing `slack_chat_reader_bot.py`

```
Fatima [2023-08-11T09:04:20] : Hey everyone, I have an urgent issue to
discuss. I just got off a call with a client who's experiencing app crashes
as soon as they load it. They're really frustrated. Can we get this sorted
ASAP? :tired_face:

Keith [2023-08-11T09:04:35] : Thanks for bringing this to our attention,
Fatima. Let's jump on this right away. John, can you take the lead in
investigating the issue since our architect is out sick today?

John [2023-08-11T09:04:52] : Sure thing, Keith. I'll dive into the codebase
and see if I can find any potential culprits for the crashes.

John [2023-08-11T09:05:30] : Fatima, could you gather some additional
information from the client? Ask them about the specific device, operating
system, and any recent updates they might have installed.

...
```

Exercises Left for the Reader

So, there are obviously a few additional things we can do here, and these steps will be left for you (the reader) to accomplish, for example:

- Connecting the code in `slack_chat_reader_bot.py` that reads the messages from Slack to the `chatgpt_client.py` so that grabbing the messages and getting a summary is a single step process.

- Adding more capabilities to the Slack bot itself such as adding commands so that anyone in the channel can request a summary. In its current state, the bot doesn't post anything in the channel. However, the "user interface" to the bot is the channel itself; therefore, someone should be able to interact with the Slack bot by typing a command (such as requesting a summary)

- Making sure that the bot doesn't make a bad situation worse. Whenever the bot provides a summary, it should not post in the channel itself because that could add a lot of noise to an already noisy situation. The best practice is to have the bot send a private message to the person asking for a summary (or whatever new command that you create).

Conclusion

In this chapter, we talked about one of the various ways artificial intelligence can be put to practical use within the enterprise today. We discussed what is truly "prompt engineering," by discussing that prompt engineering cannot be accomplished by simply textual input to ChatGPT alone. You definitely need to understand the ramifications of all the input parameters to the ChatGPT API, in order to properly, and effectively, perform prompt engineering.

Using what we learned about prompt engineering, we were able to successfully obtain summarizations of any large body of text provided to us. Finally, we saw the code necessary in order to run an automated bot that will grab messages from any Slack channel programmatically, if we specify a valid date range.

In this chapter (as well as the previous chapter), we were working exclusively with the Chat Completions model of the OpenAI APIs. In the next chapter, we're going to push the boundaries of what's possible by experimenting with the Whisper and DALL·E models.

## CHAPTER 5

Multimodal AI: Creating a Podcast Visualizer with Whisper and DALL·E 3

Now let's introduce a new term: **multimodal AI**. In the simplest of terms, generative AI models can create content in one of four formats:

- Text
- Audio
- Images
- Video

Each of those formats are a **mode**. Multimodal AI is the process of using multiple AI models together to generate (or to understand) content where the input is one type of mode and the output is a different type of mode.

Take, for example, OpenAI's Whisper model. If you provide it audio, it is able to create a transcription of everything said into text. The same thing applies to DALL·E. If you supply it with a textual prompt, then it is able to generate an image of what you described.

In this chapter, we're going to take multimodal AI to the next level! As an avid podcast listener, I've often wondered what the scenery, the imagery, the characters, the subject, or the background looked like while listening to a very immersive story in audio format.

© Lydia Evelyn, Bruce Hopkins 2024
L. Evelyn and B. Hopkins, *Beginning ChatGPT for Python*, https://doi.org/10.1007/979-8-8688-0929-3_5

So, we're going to create a Podcast Visualizer using multiple models from OpenAI. There are a few steps involved, but the final results are stunning. While listening to a podcast about a guy cooking some amazing things with tofu (don't knock it until you try it), the Podcast Visualizer came up with the image in Figure 5-1.

Figure 5-1. *The AI-Generated Result of Visualizing a Podcast About Tofu Using the GPT-4, Whisper, and DALL·E Models*

In order to make the code for the Podcast Visualizer easy to follow along, we'll do things separately in the following three steps:

- Step 1: Take a podcast episode, and use the Whisper model to get a transcript.

- Step 2: Take the resulting transcript, and use the GPT-4 model to describe the visual aspects of what's being discussed in the podcast episode.

- Step 3: Take the resulting description, and use the DALL·E model to generate an image.

The code presented here in this chapter has tons of practical uses, for example:

- If you're just curious about the things in a podcast episode could look like (which is always the case for us), you can get a simple representative visual image to associate with what you're listening to.

- For people who are hearing impaired, you can easily turn a podcast or radio program into a slideshow of images. This greatly enhances the accessibility of the content

- For podcasters, you can now have a simple way to add a visual/hero image to each of your episodes. This is useful since podcast players such as Apple Podcasts and Spotify allow podcasters to display a single image to associate with an individual episode. This can help with engagement for your listeners.

Introducing the Whisper Model by OpenAI

Now let's introduce another new term: **automatic speech recognition** (ASR). The average everyday consumer is very familiar with this technology due to its integration into mobile phones (e.g., Siri for the iPhone) and smart speakers (e.g., any Alexa device). At its core, ASR technology converts spoken language into text.

Whisper is OpenAI's model for speech recognition, and the accuracy is astonishingly high. The listing below is a transcript of an episode of the very popular Duolingo Spanish podcast, which makes the Spanish language easy to be understood by English listeners by combining both English and Spanish together in a woven narrative story. In Listing 5-1, you can see the transcript that was generated using the Whisper model.

Listing 5-1. The Whisper Model Performs Speech Recognition to Convert Audio into Text

...I'm Martina Castro. Every episode we bring you fascinating, true stories to help you improve your Spanish listening and gain new perspectives on the world. The storyteller will be using intermediate Spanish and I'll be chiming in for context in English. If you miss something, you can always skip back and listen again. We also offer full transcripts at podcast. duolingo.com.

Growing up, Linda was fascinated with her grandmother, Erlinda. Erlinda was a healer or curandera, someone who administers remedies for mental, emotional, physical, or spiritual illnesses.
In Guatemala, this is a practice passed down orally through generations in the same family. Mal de ojo, or the evil eye, is considered an illness by many Guatemalans who believe humans have the power to transfer bad energy to others. Neighbors would bring their babies to Linda's grandmother when they suspected an energy imbalance. Su madre lo llevaba a nuestra casa para curarlo...

If you've ever worked with a speech recognition system before (even with sophisticated technologies like Siri and Alexa), you will know that it has problems, for instance:

- **Speech recognition has problems with punctuation**

  - Have you noticed that nobody speaks with punctuation? For the English language, we use changes in tone or volume to ask a question or give an exclamation. We also use short and long pauses for commas and periods.

- **Speech recognition has problems with foreign words and accents**

  - Depending on who you ask, there are at least 170k words in the English language. However, in conversational English we are always using foreign words like:

    - Tsunami (Japanese origin): A large sea wave often caused by an earthquake

    - Hors d'oeuvre (French origin): An appetizer

- Lingerie (French origin): Women's underwear or nightclothes

- Aficionado (Spanish origin): Someone who is very passionate about a specific activity or subject

- Piñata (Spanish origin): A brightly colored box of candy for kids to beat relentlessly

- **Speech recognition has problems with names**

  - Certain names of people, businesses, and websites can often be hard to spell and understand

- **Speech recognition has problems with homophones**

  - Do you remember those words that sound the same but have different spellings and meanings? The fantastic editor of this book knows all of them!

    - Would / Wood

    - Flour / Flower

    - Two / Too / To

    - They're / There / Their

    - Pair / Pare / Pear

    - Break / Brake

    - Allowed / Aloud

As you can see from Listing 5-1, above, Whisper was able to understand all the punctuation in the audio, identify all the foreign words (of which there were several), understand the names, as well as the company name ("Duolingo") within a URL! Of course, if you noticed, it could also understand the difference between "wood" and "would."

Features and Limitations of the Whisper Model

The Whisper model is able to convert spoken audio from the following languages into text:

- Afrikaans
- Arabic
- Armenian
- Azerbaijani
- Belarusian
- Bosnian
- Bulgarian
- Catalan
- Chinese
- Croatian
- Czech
- Danish
- Dutch
- **English (of course!)**
- Estonian
- Finnish
- French
- Galician
- German
- Greek
- Hebrew
- Hindi
- Hungarian

- Icelandic
- Indonesian
- Italian
- Japanese
- Kannada
- Kazakh
- Korean
- Latvian
- Lithuanian
- Macedonian
- Malay
- Marathi
- Maori
- Nepali
- Norwegian
- Persian
- Polish
- Portuguese
- Romanian
- Russian
- Serbian
- Slovak
- Slovenian
- Spanish
- Swahili
- Swedish

- Tagalog

- Tamil

- Thai

- Turkish

- Ukrainian

- Urdu

- Vietnamese

- Welsh

So, at the end of the day, it will be able to understand audio spoken by yourself and probably any language spoken by your friends and colleagues.

Developers are limited to sending no more than 50 requests per minute to the API, so this constraint needs to be taken into consideration if you want to transcribe vast amounts of audio.

Whisper supports audio in flac, mp3, mp4, mpeg, mpga, m4a, ogg, wav, or webm formats. Regardless of the format that you use, the maximum file size to send to the API is 25MB.

Now, If you haven't worked extensively with audio files, please be aware that some formats create *really huge* files (e.g., wav format) and others create really small files (e.g., m4a format). So, converting your file to a different format can help you with the 25MB limitation. However, later in this chapter, we'll see the code for a tool that takes a single large audio file and splits it into multiple, smaller files.

Using `OpenAI.audio.transcriptions.create()` to Transcribe Audio

The `OpenAI.audio.transcriptions.create()` method converts audio into text and is only compatible with the Whisper model. Let's take a look at Table 5-1 to find out what needs to be in the method parameters in order to call it successfully.

Examining the Method Parameters

Table 5-1. *The Request Body for Whisper*

Field	Type	Required?	Description
file	File	Required	The entire audio file that you want to be transcribed.
			Accepted formats are
			• flac
			• mp3
			• mp4
			• mpeg
			• mpga
			• m4a
			• ogg
			• wav
			• webm
model	String	Required	The ID of the model that you want to use for transcription.
			Compatible models include
			• whisper-1
prompt	String	Optional	This is any text that can be provided to change the model's transcription style or to provide it with more context from a previous segment of audio.
			Be sure that the prompt is in the same language as the audio for best results.
			Additionally, this field can be used to change the spelling or capitalization of any words that Whisper is not familiar with.

(continued)

Table 5-1. (*continued*)

Field	Type	Required?	Description
response_format	String Default: json	Optional	This is the format of the output of transcription. Accepted formats are • json • text • srt • verbose_json • vtt
temperature	Number Default: 0	Optional	This is the sampling temperature, ranging from 0 to 1. A higher value increases the randomness of the output, whereas a lower value ensures a more deterministic output.
language	String	Optional	This is the language of the input audio. It's optional, but providing the value can improve the accuracy and latency for the transcription

Creating a Utility App to Split Audio Files: audio_splitter.py

So, we're almost at the point where we are able to programmatically invoke the Whisper model using the OpenAI.audio.transcriptions.create() method. However, the Whisper model has a limitation of 25MB per file.

Now, this is not a problem if you're listening to (for example) the *StarDate* podcast from the University of Texas at Austin. This podcast gives you a great glimpse of what to look for in the nighttime sky in about two minutes of audio. However, that's not the case for other audio programs which tend to last for up to an hour (or even more). In cases like that, you're going to definitely exceed the 25MB file limitation.

Therefore, let's pair-program with ChatGPT and use our human intelligence to create our own utility that will take a single audio file and split it into multiple smaller files.

Note   In this section, I'm presenting one of many possibilities available on how to segment a large audio file into smaller pieces. For instance, you can use popular audio editing apps (such as the Open Source tool, Audacity, or the licensed tool, Adobe Audition) to manually cut up a large file into smaller files.

FFmpeg is one of the most reliable ways to programmatically manipulate audio files, and pydub is an open source library recommended in OpenAI's documentation on using Whisper with Python.

Listing 5-2 is the prompt that is sent to ChatGPT in order to get a basic app that splits audio files.

Listing 5-2. PROMPT. Using ChatGPT to Create the audio_splitter.py App

System: You are a Python developer
User: Write an application that takes as input a single MP3 file and splits the file into contiguous segments no longer than 10 minutes using the pydub library and ffmpeg

After a little back and forth, we were able to create (as shown in Listing 5-3) the audio_splitter.py application that includes our edits to what was generated by ChatGPT.

Listing 5-3. RESPONSE. audio_splitter.py

```
from pydub import AudioSegment
import os

# Path to the input audio file
input_audio_path = "audio-example.mp3"

# Load the audio file
audio = AudioSegment.from_mp3(input_audio_path)

# Define segment length (in milliseconds) - 10 minutes
segment_length_ms = 10 * 60 * 1000  # 10 minutes in milliseconds
```

```python
# Split the audio into segments of ten minutes each
segments = [audio[i:i+segment_length_ms] for i in range(0, len(audio),
segment_length_ms)]

# Output directory for saving segments
output_directory = "/PATH/TO/OUTPUT"

# Ensure output directory exists, create it if necessary
os.makedirs(output_directory, exist_ok=True)

# Process each segment (for example, you can save them to separate files)
for i, segment in enumerate(segments):
    segment.export(os.path.join(output_directory, f"segment_{i}.mp3"),
    format="mp3")
```

Our goal is simple: split an MP3 file into contiguous segments no longer than ten minutes using the Python language. In this process, we follow these steps:

- Specify the input file path, output directory, and the desired segment duration in milliseconds (ten minutes).

- Load the MP3 file using the pydub library's AudioSegment class, which provides functionalities for audio processing.

- Iterate through the input MP3 file, segmenting it into smaller parts of the specified duration (ten minutes or less) using slicing.

- Save each segment as a separate MP3 file in the specified output directory.

In order for this to work, you need to have the pydub library **and** FFmpeg properly installed and configured in your project. FFmpeg is an extremely versatile media converter which not only handles MP3 audio files, but various other audio file formats (including m4a, ogg, and wav). It is able to convert video formats as well as static images like png, jpeg, and gif.

After running the script, you'll have a folder full of segmented audio files that are ten minutes long or less. Using the `audio_splitter.py` utility, you have a simple to use Python script to modify the settings that work best for you. For our purposes, the goal here is to have audio files that are <25MB, so if you're transcribing eight-hour legal proceedings (for example) in WAV format, you may need to adjust the duration to be shorter, like six minutes in length.

When using the audio splitter, the best practice is to have the output folder to be a different folder from the input, and you'll see why when we start to invoke the OpenAI `audio.transcriptions.create()` method using the Whisper model.

Creating the Audio Transcriber: `whisper_transcriber.py`

Now, let's build our next Python app, `whisper_transcriber.py`. Again, we're going to pair-program with ChatGPT to get a basis to work with. Listing 5-4 is the prompt to put in the Chat Playground to get things started.

Listing 5-4. PROMPT. Asking ChatGPT to Use OpenAI's Python Library and Send MP3 Files to Whisper's API

System: You are a Python developer.
User: Using Python, write a script that iterates over all of the mp3 files in a single folder on my local computer and send all the files in the folder to be transcribed by OpenAI's Whisper model, using the OpenAI's python library.

Model: gpt-4o

Temperature: 1

Maximum Length: 1150

After some back and forth, Listing 5-5 shows the response ChatGPT gave us that worked.

Listing 5-5. RESPONSE. whisper_transcriber.py

```
import os
import openai
from dotenv import load_dotenv
```

```python
def transcribe_mp3_files(openai_api_key, mp3_folder_path):
    # Set OpenAI API key
    openai.api_key = openai_api_key

    # Model used for transcription
    model = "whisper-1"

    # Desired format for the transcription response
    response_format = "text"

    # Iterate over each MP3 file in the folder
    for filename in sorted(os.listdir(mp3_folder_path)):
        if filename.endswith(".mp3"):
            file_path = os.path.join(mp3_folder_path, filename)
            try:
                # Read the content of the MP3 file
                with open(file_path, "rb") as f:
                    file_content = f.read()

                # Transcribe the MP3 file
                response = openai.audio.transcriptions.create(
                    file=(filename, file_content),
                    model=model,
                    response_format=response_format
                )
                # Print the entire response object
                print(response)
            except Exception as e:
                print(f"Transcription error for file {filename}: {e}")

def main():
    # Load environment variables from .env file
    load_dotenv()

    # API key for OpenAI
    openai_api_key = os.getenv("OPENAI_API_KEY")
```

```
# Folder containing the MP3 files to be transcribed
mp3_folder_path = "/PATH/TO/OUTPUT"   # Replace with your MP3
folder path

# Transcribe MP3 files
transcribe_mp3_files(openai_api_key, mp3_folder_path)
```
```
if __name__ == "__main__":
    main()
```

As you can see from the code listing above, one of the major benefits of keeping the input file in a separate folder from the output files is that you can give the script above the path to the output folder and you don't have to worry about anything else. This script will grab all the files in the output folder regardless of the number of files in that folder, so it could be one or 100 files – it doesn't matter.

Having a Little Fun and Trying Things Out with a Podcast

Ok, so let's run a test using the code that we have presented so far. *This American Life* is a weekly public radio program (and also a podcast) that's hosted by Ira Glass and produced in collaboration with WBEZ Chicago. The icon for this podcast is shown in Figure 5-2.

Figure 5-2. *If You're Looking for a Good Podcast with Compelling Stories, I Recommend Listening to "This American Life" (Image credit: WBEZ Chicago)*

Each episode weaves together a series of stories centered around a specific theme or topic. Some stories are investigative journalism, and others are simply interviews with ordinary people with captivating stories. Episode 811 is entitled, "The one place I can't go." and the file is 56MB in MP3 format. Since we already know that 56MB is way too big to send to Whisper to get transcribed, we need the audio_splitter.py to break up the file for us.

Listing 5-6 shows an excerpt from the full transcript of the episode.

Listing 5-6. The Partial Transcript of Episode 811 of "This American Life"

"...My younger cousin Camille is not really a dog person, but there is one dog she adored. Her name was Foxy, because she looked exactly like a fox, except she was black. She was the neighbor's dog, but she and Camille seemed to have a real kinship, maybe because they both weren't very far from the ground. Camille was around four or five years old back then, and she had a little lisp, so Foxy came out as Fozzie. I thought it was one of the cutest things I'd ever heard.

The way Camille remembers Foxy, it's almost like a movie. Her memories feel like endless summer, hazy and perfect, like a scene shot on crackly film. I just remembered like the feeling of being excited to go and see Foxy. I have an image in my head of like coming to the house, and I could see Foxy was like outside. I can see Foxy through the door that leads to the garden. There's a story about Camille and Foxy that I think about fairly often. I've talked about it with my sister for years, but never with Camille. And it's this. Once when they were playing..."

For brevity, we're only showing an excerpt of the transcript. The full transcript itself is over 8000 words due to the fact that the episode is nearly one hour in length.

Going Meta: Prompt Engineering GPT-4 to Write a Prompt for DALL·E

Since the full text transcript of the podcast episode that we want to visualize is thousands of words, we're going to use GPT-4 to automatically create the prompt needed for the DALL·E model. DALL·E is able to take a textual description in a prompt and create an image, but it's best to keep the prompt as short as possible. Listing 5-7 is the prompt for GPT-4 to generate a prompt for DALL·E.

Listing 5-7. The Prompt for GPT-4 to Create a Prompt for DALL·E

System: You are a service that helps to visualize podcasts.
User: Read the following transcript from a podcast. Describe for a visually impaired person the background and subject that best represents the overall theme of the episode. Start with any of the following phrases:
- "A photo of"
- "A painting of"
- "A macro 35mm photo of"
- "Digital art of "

User: Support for This American Life comes from Squarespace...
Model: gpt-4o
Temperature: 1.47
Maximum length: 150
Top P: 0
Frequency penalty: 0.33
Presence penalty: 0

DALL·E needs to know the type of image to generate so that's why we need to specify that the image should be a photo, painting, digital art, etc. We need to ensure that the resulting text generated by GPT-4 is short, so we want to have a maximum length of 150 tokens. Also, in order to prevent GPT-4 from repeating some phrases multiple times, we introduced a frequency penalty of 0.33.

Listing 5-8 shows the results from GPT-4 after reading the transcript of Episode 811 of *This American Life*.

Listing 5-8. The Prompt for DALL·E Created by GPT-4

Digital art of a young girl sitting in a garden with a black dog that looks like a fox. The girl is smiling and the dog is wagging its tail. The image has a hazy, dream-like quality, with crackly film effects to evoke nostalgia.

Using **OpenAI.images.generate()** to Create Images

In order to use the DALL·E model to dynamically create an image from a text prompt, you need to call the OpenAI.images.generate() method.

Examining the Method Parameters

Table 5-2 describes the format of the parameter necessary for the request body for the `OpenAI.images.generate()` method. For obvious reasons, the prompt parameter is the only required parameter in order to successfully invoke the model.

Table 5-2. *Request Body for the OpenAI.images.generate() method*

Field	Type	Required?	Description
prompt	String	Required	This is where you describe the image that you want to be created.
			The maximum length is 1000 characters for dall-e-2 and 4000 characters for dall-e-3.
model	String	Optional	The model name to generate the image.
			Compatible models include
			• "dall-e-2"
			• "dall-e-3"
n	Integer or null Default: 1	Optional	This is the requested number of images that you want created.
			Must be between 1 and 10.
			Note: Due to the complexity required for dall-e-3, OpenAI may limit your request to a single image.
quality	String Default: "standard"	Optional	This allows you to specify the quality of the image to be generated. This parameter is only valid for dall-e-3.
			Accepted values are
			• "standard"
			• "hd"

(continued)

Table 5-2. (*continued*)

Field	Type	Required?	Description
size	String or null Default: "1024x1024"	Optional	The size of the generated images. Image sizes available for dall-e-2 are • "256x256" • "512x512" • "1024x1024" Image sizes available for dall-e-3 are • "1024x1024" • "1792x1024" (landscape) • "1024x1792" (portrait)
style	String Default: "vivid"	Optional	This allows you to specify how natural-looking the generated image should be. This parameter is only valid for dall-e-3. Accepted values are • "natural" (good for photos) • "vivid" (good for artistic looks)
response_format	String or null Default: "url"	Optional	This is the format of the generated image. Accepted values are • "url" • "b64_json"
user	String	Optional	This is a unique identifier representing your end-user, which can help OpenAI to monitor and detect abuse.

Handling the Response

After successfully invoking the OpenAI.images.generate() method, the API will respond with an image JSON object. Table 5-3 shows a breakdown of the image object, which only has one parameter.

Table 5-3. *The Structure of the Response Object*

Field	Type	Description
url (or) b64_json	String	This is a url to your generated image if the response_format is "url" in the request. (or) This is a base64-encoded JSON image if the response_format is "b64_json" in the request.

Creating the Image Generator: `dalle_client.py`

Listing 5-9 is a short and sweet script that allows us to programmatically invoke DALL·E in order to create any image that we want.

Listing 5-9. Using DALL·E with Python in dalle_client.py

```python
import openai
import os
from dotenv import load_dotenv

# Load API key from .env file
load_dotenv()
api_key = os.getenv("OPENAI_API_KEY")
openai.api_key = api_key

# Define prompt and size
prompt = "a 35mm macro photo of 3 cute Rottweiler puppies with no collars
laying down in a field"
size = "1024x1024"

# Generate image using DALL·E
response = openai.images.generate(
```

121

```
    prompt=prompt,
    size=size,
    model="dall-e-3"
)
print("Image URL:", response.data[0].url)
```

Figures 5-3 and 5-4 below show the images generated from the text prompt in Listing 5-8 from the podcast episode 811 of *This American Life*.

Figure 5-3. *The DALL·E-Generated Image of a Girl and Her Dog from Episode 811 of "This American Life" Podcast*

Figure 5-4. *The DALL·E-Generated Image of a Girl and Her Dog from Episode 811 of "This American Life" Podcast*

DALL·E Prompt Engineering and Best Practices

Now, creating images with DALL·E takes prompt engineering in order to get consistent, desired results, and it's a good idea to play around with different prompts to get some practice to see what works for you and your use case. Maybe you prefer paintings instead of 3D-looking images? Maybe you need photos instead of digital art? Maybe you want the image to be a close-up shot instead of a portrait? There are a lot of possibilities to consider.

Regardless of your use case, here are two golden rules in order to get the most out of your DALL·E prompts.

DALL·E Golden Rule #1: Get Familiar with the Types of Images That DALL·E Can Generate

First and foremost, one of the most important things that DALL·E needs to understand is the type of image that needs to be generated. Here's a list of several of the most common types of images that DALL·E is able to create:

- 3D render

- Painting

- Abstract painting

- Expressive oil painting

- Oil painting (in the style of any deceased artist)

- Oil pastel

- Digital art

- Photo

- Photorealistic

- Hyperrealistic

- Neon photo

- 35-mm macro photo

- High-quality photo

- Silhouette

- Vaporware

- Cartoon

- Plush object

- Marble sculpture

- Hand sketch

- Poster

- Pencil and watercolor

- Synth wave

- Comic book style

- Hand drawn

DALL·E Golden Rule #2: Be Descriptive with What You Want in the Foreground and Background

We cannot emphasize enough that you need to be descriptive with DALL·E in order to get consistent, desirable results. It may sound weird, but the best way to describe your image to DALL·E is to act like you're describing a dream to another person.

So, as a mental exercise between us, try to describe your last dream. As you describe the people, places, and things in your dream, you have in your mind the most important things that you remember, as well as the experience that you felt. As you describe things to another person, tiny details start to emerge such as

- How many people were present (if any)?

- What position were the people or animals in? Standing, sitting, or laying down?

- What things were in the scenery and the background?

- What items stood out to you? Sounds? Smells? Colors?

- How did you feel? Happy, eerie, excited?

- What was the perceived time of day? Morning, midday, night?

If you can describe a dream to another person, then you should have no problem describing what you want to DALL·E.

Let's Play Around with Prompts to DALL·E

To give you an idea of what kind of things you can do with DALL·E, we've created a couple prompts for images in a variety of styles for inspiration to get you started. Figures 5-5 through 5-10 show several different examples.

Figure 5-5. *Photo-Realistic: Penguin at an Office Desk*

Figure 5-6. *Vector Art: A Man Wearing Sunglasses with a Beard of Flowers*

Figure 5-7. *Vaporwave: Greek Statues in a Temple*

Figure 5-8. *Digital Painting: A Female Videogame Character in a Jungle with a Spear and a Shield*

Figure 5-9. *3D Art: A Baby Panda Working at a Typewriter*

Figure 5-10. *Oil Painting: Ship on Stormy Water with Dynamic Lighting and Lightning in the Background*

Conclusion

In this chapter, we accomplished a lot! With a few scripts, we created a Podcast Visualizer.

- We created and used `audio_splitter.py`, which works as a utility for us. If you have an audio file that's larger than the limitations of the Whisper model, this script will give you a folder of smaller audio files to send to Whisper.

- We created and used `whisper_transcriber.py` to get a transcription of a folder of audio files. The folder can contain a single audio file or several files. Your only limitation is the number of requests that you can send to the Whisper model.

- We did a little prompt engineering with GPT-4 in order to get a descriptive prompt of the imagery in a podcast based upon the transcript.

- Finally, we created and used `dalle_client.py` to take the prompt generated from calling the GPT-4 model and getting an image that represents the podcast episode visually.

Exercises Left for the Reader

So, there are obviously a few additional things we can do here, and these steps will be left for you (the reader) to accomplish, for example:

- The `audio_splitter.py` app is a Python interface to FFmpeg. FFmpeg can not only split audio files but can also do a lot more with media files, such as format conversion and reencoding. Experiment to see which of the supported media formats by Whisper are the smallest audio files. Hint: It's definitely not wav format.

- If you're planning to create an app or a service that automatically generates images based upon a textual prompt from your end-users, then you definitely would want to update the `dalle_client.py` script in order to ensure that you're tracking and providing in your request the user parameter. This is due to the fact that your end-user has the potential to generate harmful images through your API key. Remember, you have an API account with Open AI, and they don't! As a result, you need to be aware if you need to terminate your business relationship with a user who is violating Open AI content rules through your service.

## CHAPTER 6

Creating an Automated Community Manager Bot with Discord and Python

When you're launching an app or a service, it's important to build and maintain your own community. Below are the telltale signs of a healthy user community:

- Members engage in meaningful discussions, sharing insights, feedback, and support.

- Disagreements or debates occur, but they are approached constructively without resorting to personal attacks or derogatory language.

- There's an atmosphere of respect, where members listen to each other and acknowledge differing opinions.

- A mix of old and new members actively participate, ensuring the community remains vibrant and doesn't stagnate.

- Users contribute diverse content, from answering questions to sharing resources, which enriches the community's knowledge base.

- There's a balance between giving and taking; members who seek help or information also offer it to others.

- New members frequently join, often referred by existing members, indicating that the community is seen positively and worth recommending.

© Lydia Evelyn, Bruce Hopkins 2024
L. Evelyn and B. Hopkins, *Beginning ChatGPT for Python*, https://doi.org/10.1007/979-8-8688-0929-3_6

- Users often become advocates for the community or platform, promoting it outside of the direct community space, such as on social media or other forums.

- The community helps to shape the app or service by providing new ideas for features and functionality

No matter what type of app or service that I create, I would love for my user community to exemplify the items listed above!

Choosing Discord as Your Community Platform

Over the past few years, Discord has surged in popularity as a useful tool for community management for people who are passionate about their communities. This is partially due to its cross-platform compatibility, allowing members to stay connected whether they're on a desktop, mobile device, or web browser. However, one of its standout features is the invitation-based community system, which helps community managers to control growth and prevents spam. This model not only ensures a tailored experience for members but also enhances security, since community managers have the discretion to grant or deny access.

Discord not only supports text messaging but also supports voice chats and streaming video. Very similar to Slack, Discord allows community managers to separate content into channels to organize discussions, streamline information flow, and help users see the content that they're interested in.

Creating a More Advanced Bot Than Our Slack Bot

Now, If you successfully went through the steps in Chapter 4 where we worked with a Slack bot, then the steps in this chapter will feel familiar to you. In Chapter 4, we created a Slack bot to read a single channel during a time period and get a summary of the content discussed. The Slack bot was not a community manager but was more like a helpful assistant.

For the remainder of this book, we're going to perform all the steps necessary to make powerful bots for Discord that will use AI to help actually manage the community.

Creating a More Advanced Bot Than Any Typical Discord Bot

If you've ever had any experience using a Discord bot, then you're probably aware that the most common way in order to interact with them is with what's called a "/command." This enables typical bots (read: nonintelligent bots) to essentially work only when they have received a very specific operation or command. If the "/command" is not provided, then the bot will be silent and not do anything. Essentially, it exemplifies the phrase "speak only when you are spoken to."

However, we are creating a Discord bot that will be artificially intelligent, and therefore, it will be much more advanced than any typical Discord bot. We're going to create bots that will be able to read and see all messages in the Discord server and be intelligent enough to respond correctly.

Understanding the Roles for the Bots

So, let's explore a scenario in order to make things real. We're creating a public Discord server to interact with the users of a mobile banking app. Our end goal is to have bots written in Python to handle the following scenarios:

- Q&A: Monitor a specific channel and automatically answer questions from users about how to use the banking app. For this to work, the bot will need to be trained on how the app works

- No solicitations: For any business community, it's important that the participants of the community are not being targeted by unscrupulous individuals. For example, if you're creating a banking app, do you want your customers contacted by anyone whose username is "B4nk Admin"?

- No harmful content: For any community, it's important for the members to be protected from harmful content such as hate language

Our Example Bank: Crook's Bank

For the purposes of this example, I decided upon a fictional name of a fictional bank that would have an extremely low likelihood of coinciding with the name of a real bank. Therefore, for this example, "Crook's Bank" is launching a new mobile app for customers of their bank. They want to have a channel that will be monitored by a bot to answer questions from users of the app, and they also want to ensure that no one is soliciting users of their app or posting hurtful or harmful content in their Discord servers. Figure 6-1 shows a fun illustration of Crook's Bank.

Figure 6-1. *This Fake App from a Fake Bank Has Real Problems*

First Things First: Create Your Own Discord Server

Before we can make an AI Discord bot, we're obviously going to need a Discord server already in place for the bot to interact with. Use either the Discord App or go to the Discord website (log in first of course), and start the process to Add/Create a new server.

After you have started the process, select the option labeled "Create My Own" as shown in Figure 6-2.

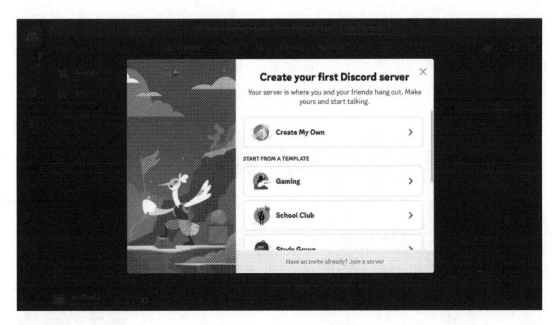

Figure 6-2. *Creating Your Own Discord Server*

Next, you'll be prompted to specify additional information about your server. Continue to proceed through the creation process until you are prompted to provide a name and icon for your server, as shown in Figure 6-3.

Specify the name of your server and provide an optional server icon (if you have one).

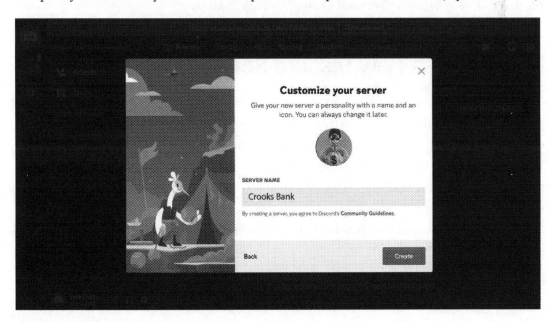

Figure 6-3. *Providing a Name for Your Own Discord Server*

Create the Q&A Channel

By default, every Discord server has a "general" channel, but we want a dedicated channel especially for questions and answers. Depending upon how you created your server, Figure 6-4 will be presented to you to create your new channel.

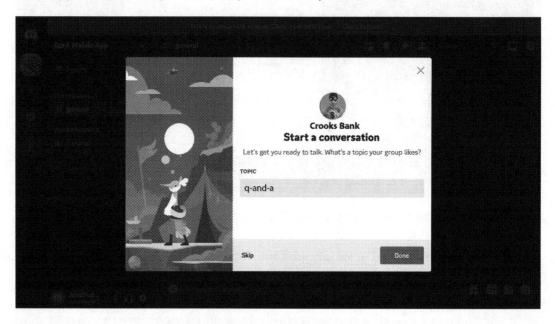

Figure 6-4. *Creating a Channel Using the Web Interface*

Registering a New Discord Bot App with Discord

Now that we have our Discord server with the appropriate channels created, it's time to register the bot itself – or rather, in our case, the bots themselves. In order to keep the code clean and manageable, we'll actually have multiple bots for our Discord server. The first bot will be used exclusively to answer questions in the "q-and-a" channel. The second bot will monitor all channels for unwanted content, such as harmful content or solicitations.

In order to create our bot, head over to the Discord Developers website, which is also shown in Figure 6-5:

```
https://discord.com/developers
```

Figure 6-5. *In Order to Create a Discord Bot, Go To the Discord Developers Website*

At the top-right of the page, click on the button "New Application," as shown in Figure 6-5.

In both Discord and Slack terminology, a "bot" is an "app," and bots are not allowed to run on Discord servers unless they have been registered with Discord first.

Specify a name for the bot and click the "Create" button, as shown in Figure 6-6.

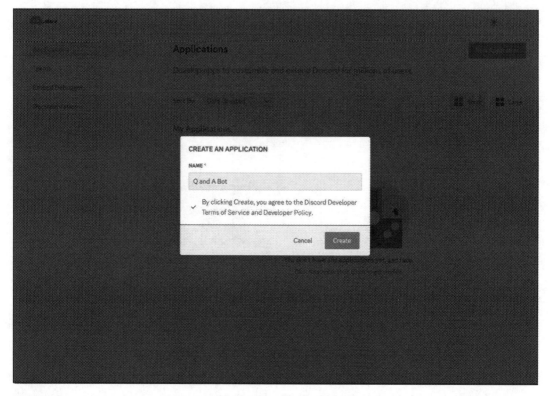

Figure 6-6. *Creating/Registering a Bot for Discord*

Specifying General Info for the Bot

Afterward, you will be taken to a page where you can specify general information about your bot, as shown in Figure 6-7.

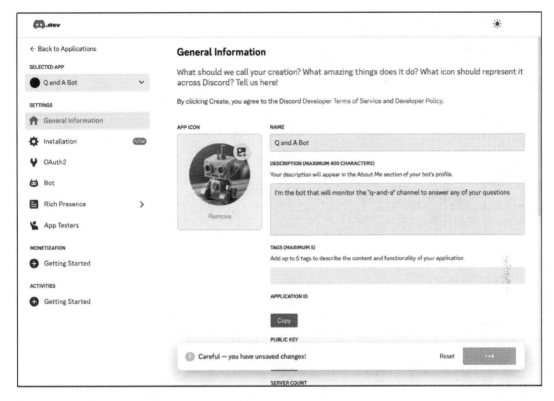

Figure 6-7. *I Decided to Give My Bot a Cute Little Robot Icon*

Be sure to familiarize yourself with the navigation menu on the left side of the page. As you can see, we have several categories of settings to configure for our bot. By default, we have landed on the "General Information" page, where we specify basic info about our bot. If you have an icon ready for your bot, you can upload it here.

Specifying OAuth2 Parameters for the Bot

Now, it's time to specify the scopes and permissions for our bot. If you followed the steps in creating a Slack bot in Chapter 4, then (as stated before) this procedure will feel familiar to you. Bots **cannot** and **should not** have the ability to do anything and everything – they should be only allowed to perform a list of operations that they were designed to perform.

On the settings navigation menu on the left, navigate to "OAuth2 > OAuth2 URL Generator" to continue.

Below are the scopes that we want:

- Scopes

    - Bot

This is reflected in Figure 6-8.

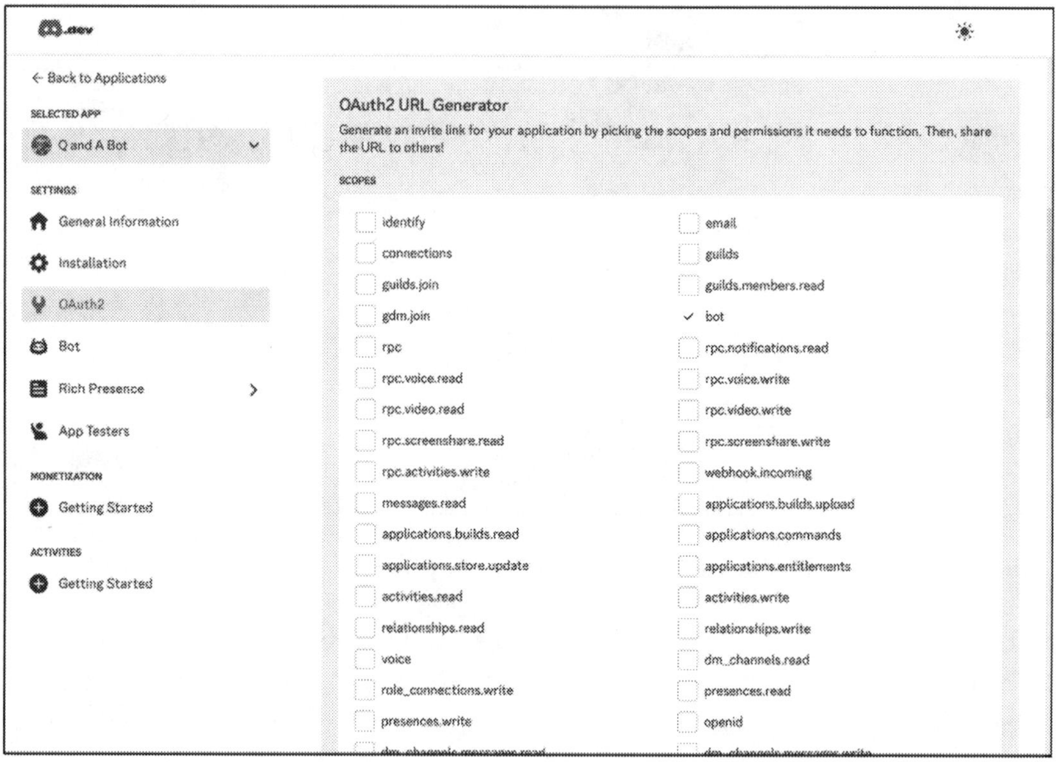

Figure 6-8. *Selecting the Scopes*

After we select the bot's scope, we get to see all the permissions that are only applicable to bots (be sure to scroll down to see them).

Bots can be pretty powerful depending on the permissions you give it. There are permissions that allow the bot to act in the capacity of a normal human moderator, such as managing the server, roles, and channels. Bots with these permissions can also kick and ban members.

What we're going to enable for our bot right now are the ones that allow the bot to send and receive messages in text channels, and voice permissions allow the bot to participate in voice channels. Simple enough, right?

Select the following permissions for the bot:

- Bot permissions

  - Read messages/view channels

  - Send messages

  - Read message history

This is reflected in Figure 6-9.

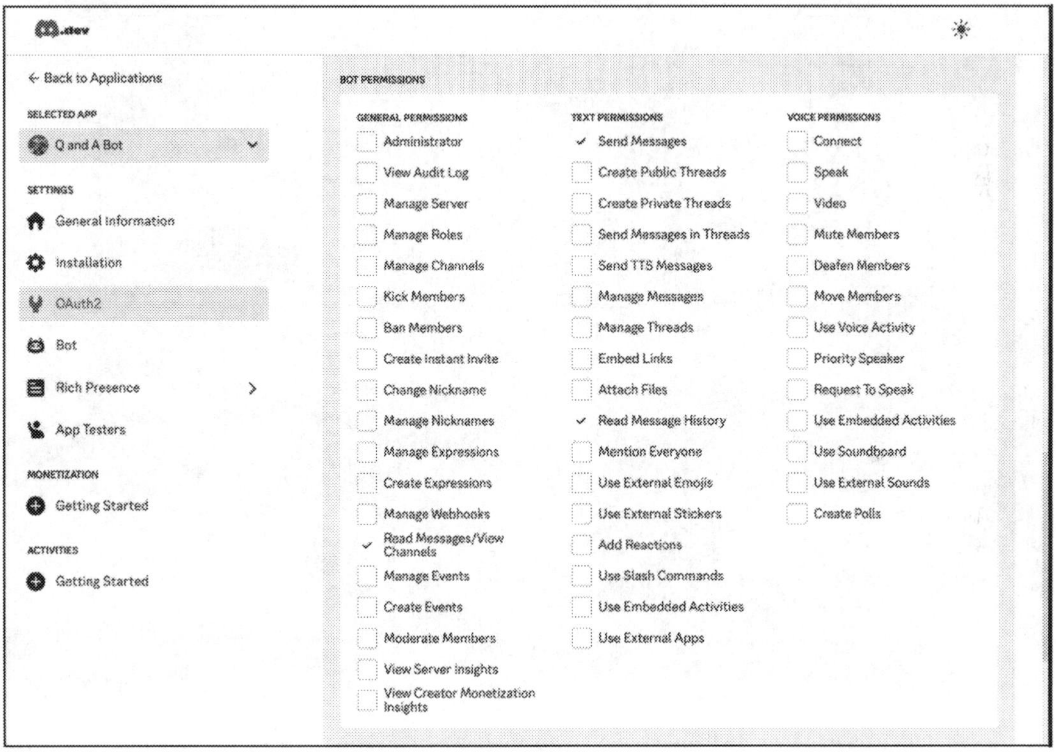

Figure 6-9. *Specifying the Bot Permissions*

Although you haven't written any Python code yet, now it's time to invite your bot to your server.

Invite Your Bot to Your Server

After you have selected the appropriate permissions, Discord will give you a dynamically generated URL that will enable you to invite your bot to your server (scroll down on the page in case you don't see it).

Copy the URL and paste it into a web browser where you're already authenticated into Discord. The result is shown in Figure 6-10.

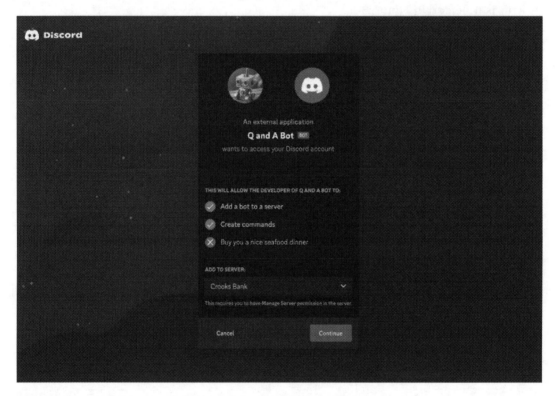

Figure 6-10. *If You Read the Screen Carefully Here, You Can See That Discord Has a Sense of Humor*

Click the "Continue" button to add the bot to your server.

Next, you will see a page that looks quite similar to the previous one, but the main difference is that it will give you a summary of all the permissions and capabilities of the bot. Typically, this is quite useful if you are adding a bot to a server that you *did not create*. However, since we created this bot ourselves, this is just a confirmation of the settings that we have already specified earlier. Figure 6-11 shows the confirmation screen for authorizing our bot with the selected permissions.

Figure 6-11. *Confirming the Capabilities of the Bot*

Click on the "Authorize" button to give the bot the permission to run on your server.

If everything went smoothly, then you should see an automated message in the general channel of your server that indicates that the process has been successful.

Getting the Discord ID Token for Your Bot and Setting the Gateway Intents

Now, it's time to get the Discord ID token for your bot, which you'll use in your code to authenticate your bot programmatically.

Note   For obvious reasons, using the word "token" here makes me nervous because this word has two distinct meanings in this book due to the context, but here's a quick refresher on the meanings:

- When using Discord and Slack APIs, a "token" is an authentication token.

- When using OpenAI APIs, a "token" as a part of a word.

Go back to the Discord Developers website, and click the "Bot" category in the settings navigation menu to continue.

Although you haven't seen your token yet, you need to click the "Reset Token" button, as shown in Figure 6-12.

Be sure to copy and save the ID token to someplace safe. You will need this token in the Python code that's presented later in this chapter.

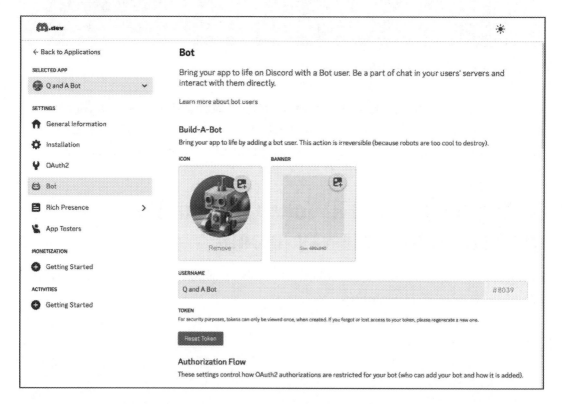

Figure 6-12. *Click on the "Reset Token" Button to See Your ID Token*

Scroll down the page to the section named "Privileged Gateway Intents" and enable the option named "MESSAGE CONTENT INTENT."

Note   So, let's slow things down a bit and talk about intents. What exactly is an "intent" and why is it needed? For the purposes of the Discord API, you need to specify explicitly every type of information that you want to be notified by Discord programmatically. Otherwise, Discord will constantly bombard you with events that are not relevant to you or your bot. For example, for our purposes, we don't care when people join or leave the server. However, if you want to send a list of server rules to anyone who joins your server for the first time, then you definitely would want to enable the "SERVER MEMBERS INTENT." When we deep dive into the code, you'll see more information about intents.

Be sure to click on the green button, "Save Changes" to save your changes. The result is shown in Figure 6-13.

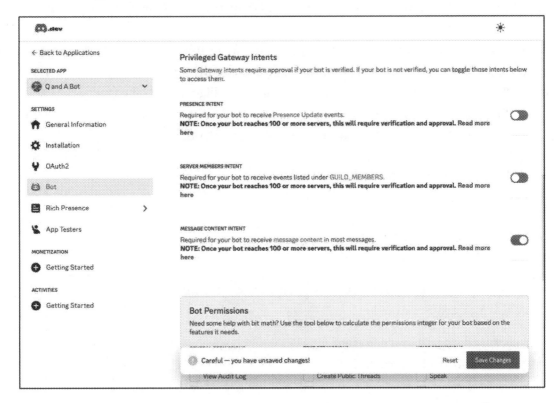

Figure 6-13. *Enable the option named "MESSAGE CONTENT INTENT"*

Creating a Q&A Bot App in Python to Answer Questions from a Channel: tech_support_bot_dumb.py

Of course, now that we've done all the prerequisites necessary and we know the name of the channel that we want to monitor for questions from our users, let's get to the code in Python that joins our server and accesses all the messages from a specific Discord channel.

This is the first of two Discord bots that we're creating in this chapter. This bot, tech_support_bot_dumb.py, will be responsible for watching the messages in the "q-and-a" channel in our Discord server.

Later on, in this chapter, we'll create another bot that will be responsible for moderating *all content* in the Discord server for unwanted content, including the "q-and-a" channel. The goal here is to follow the architectural pattern of "separation of concerns." Rather than creating a gigantic Python Discord bot that performs all the moderation needs for the Discord server, we're going to separate the functionality into two different apps.

We're also going to take things step by step and focus this chapter on getting past the learning curve for the Discord capabilities in Python. In the final chapters of this book, we'll enhance both bots and make them artificially intelligent using the Open AI APIs.

Listing 6-1 is the code that we need to create a basic Discord bot that watches all the messages posted in a single channel and provides an answer.

Listing 6-1. *tech_support_bot_dumb.py*

```
import discord

# Bot's token for authentication
discord_token = 'YOUR_TOKEN_HERE'

# Name of the channel the bot should monitor and interact with
channel_to_watch = 'q-and-a'

# Initialize the Discord client
discord_client = discord.Client()
```

```python
# Event handler for when the bot is ready
@discord_client.event
async def on_ready():
    print('Logged in as', client.user)
    print('------')

# Event handler for when a message is received
@ discord_client.event
async def on_message(message):
    # Ignore messages sent by the bot to prevent self-responses
    if message.author == client.user:
        return

    # Ignore messages not in the specified "q-and-a" channel
    if isinstance(message.channel, discord.TextChannel) and message.
channel.name != channel_to_watch:
        return

    # Send a greeting response to the user who sent the message
    reply = f'hi {message.author.mention}, I can help you with that!'
    await message.channel.send(reply)

# Run the bot with the provided token
discord_client.run(discord_token)
```

At the beginning of the script, you should notice that we specify the channel that we are interested in monitoring with the "channel_to_watch" variable.

Note   For some reason, Discord's own terminology sometimes refers to Discord servers as "guilds." However, from our perspective, a guild is simply a Discord server.

Handling Messages Sent to the Discord Server

As we wrap things up for this first Python Discord bot, we need to talk about the on_message(message) function. This function is called asynchronously for every single message sent to the Discord server, as well as for messages from users sent directly to the bot itself as a DM.

Note   Did you know that when the bot sends an answer to a person's question in the Discord server, Discord will invoke the on_message(message) function of the bot to give the bot the message that the bot just sent. This sounds like a recipe for an infinite loop, doesn't it? Therefore, we have logic in place for the bot to ignore messages sent from itself.

In the final lines of the on_message(message) function, we make sure that we give a friendly reply to the original sender of the message by "tagging" them in the response. As we mentioned before, this first version of the Q&A bot is dumb. It will respond to your question when posted in the Discord server, but the response won't actually answer your question.

Success! Running Your First Discord Bot: tech_support_bot_dumb.py

Now, let's run our Python Discord bot. After executing the app, be sure to return back to your Discord server and try to type a question in the channel that you set up for Q&A. Figure 6-14 shows the response to my question, "Is this bot going to answer my questions about the app?"

Figure 6-14. *Success Running the Q&A Bot in Discord*

As you carefully inspect Figure 6-14, you'll see some key features such as

- On the right side, you'll see that the bot is online with a green status indicator.

- After asking a question in the channel, the bot will tag you directly.

Streamlining the Process of Registering Our Next Discord Bot App with Discord

Now that we have successfully performed all the steps in order to get a functioning Discord bot, creating the second bot will be a piece of cake! So, let's briefly reiterate all the steps from above in order to create our second Discord bot. I'll be sure to point out the items that need to be changed or enhanced due to the fact that this second bot will work as a moderator, instead of providing answers to questions from the users of our Discord server.

Registering a New Discord Bot App with Discord

Perform the same steps as above; however, it would be wise to give the bot a different name. For me, this second bot will be named "Mod Bot."

Specifying General Info for the Bot

For me, I have a different icon for the content moderator bot, so I specified it here, as you can see in Figure 6-15.

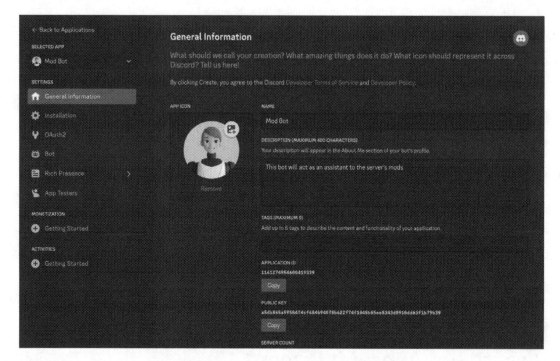

Figure 6-15. *Providing a Name and Icon for the Second Bot*

Specifying OAuth2 Parameters for the Bot

This second bot needs more permissions in order to perform more tasks. Below are the scopes that we want:

- Bot

  - Kick members

  - Ban members

  - Send messages

  - Manage messages

  - Read message history

Invite Your Bot to Your Server

Repeat the same steps as above for the first bot.

Getting the Discord ID Token for Your Bot and Setting the Gateway Intents

Again, follow the steps above in order to get the Discord ID token. Then, scroll down the page to the section named "Privileged Gateway Intents," and enable the options named "SERVER MEMBERS INTENT" and "MESSAGE CONTENT INTENT."

Creating The Next Discord Bot: content_moderator_bot_dumb.py

The role of the content moderator is to make sure that unwanted content is not posted in the Discord server. Just like the previous bot that we created earlier in this chapter, this bot will not (yet) be artificially intelligent. In its current state, the bot will indiscriminately delete any message posted anywhere in the server that contains the word "puppies."

It's not because puppies are inherently evil. However, they do have a tendency to destroy your favorite pair of shoes when left alone. In all honesty, we simply need something to test our code in Discord when we run our bot.

Listing 6-2 is the code for content_moderator_bot_dumb.py.

Listing 6-2. content_moderator_bot_dumb.py

```python
import discord

# Bot's token for authentication
discord_token = ''

# Banned word to monitor in messages
banned_word = 'puppies'

# Initialize the Discord client
discord_client = discord.Client()
```

```python
# Event handler for when the bot is ready
@discord_client.event
async def on_ready():
    print('Logged in as', discord_client.user)
    print('------')

# Event handler for when a message is received
@discord_client.event
async def on_message(message):
    # Ignore messages sent by the bot to prevent self-responses
    if message.author == discord_client.user:
        return

    # Check if the message was sent in a guild (server)
    if message.guild is not None:
        # Check if the banned word is in the message content
        if banned_word in message.content:
            # Delete the message
            await message.delete()

            # Mention the user who sent the inappropriate message
            author_mention = message.author.mention

            # Send a warning message mentioning the user
            await message.channel.send(f'{author_mention} This comment was
deemed inappropriate for this channel. '
                                       'If you believe this to be in error,
                                       please contact one of the human
                                       server moderators.')

# Run the bot with the provided token
discord_client.run(discord_token)
```

Handling Messages Sent to the Discord Server

Again, let's focus our attention on the onMessageReceived() function, since it's called asynchronously every time a message is posted to the Discord server. As you can see, if the message posted to the server contains the banned word, then we delete the message and warn the sender with a @mention message in the same channel where the offending message was posted.

Success Again! Running Your Second Discord Bot: content_moderator_bot_dumb.py

Now, let's run our second Python Discord bot. After executing the app, be sure to return back to your Discord server and type a message in any channel that contains the offending word. Figure 6-16 shows the bot in action.

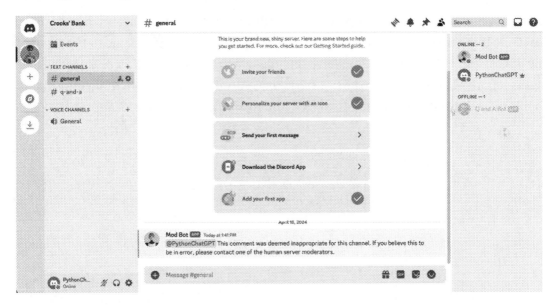

Figure 6-16. *This Bot Has a Strict Rule About Discussing "Puppies"; However, Discussing "Kittens" Is Perfectly Fine*

Conclusion

We just went through all the steps necessary to create two functioning Discord bots in Python. For those who are unfamiliar with the process of creating a Discord server, we showed the process on how to set up a server to manage our community.

As you can see, we took a much different approach compared to our Slack bot that we did in Chapter 4! The Slack bot that we created was pretty much focused on user productivity within the workplace. The two Discord bots, on the other hand, are truly focused on community management. We have everything in place for these bots to be artificially intelligent with the help of OpenAI's APIs. This is all accomplished in the final two chapters.

Exercises Left for the Reader

In the next chapters, we're going to make our "dumb" bots to be intelligent, but there's at least one thing we can do right now. Rather than using the command line to report status messages, it's better for the bots to have their own channel that's exclusively used for status reports. This way, when the bot starts up, shuts down, or has anything important to inform the administrators, it's all logged and recorded in a central location.

CHAPTER 7

Adding Intelligence to Our Discord Bots, Part 1: Using the Chat Model for Q&A

At this point, we have all the structure in place to make both our Discord bots that we created in the previous chapter to be fully functional and artificially intelligent, and that's what we're going to do in the final chapters of this book. The focus of this chapter will be on our tech support bot, which was called `tech_support_bot_dumb.py`. Below are the two major changes that we're going to make:

- Modify our `chatgpt_client.py` script so that the Discord bot script can ask questions about specific information that we provide to it. The updated file will be a class called chatgpt_client_for_qa_and_ moderation.py. It will be used for Q&A purposes in this chapter but will be used in the final chapter of the book as well.

- Modify our `tech_support_bot.py` script (formerly named, `tech_ support_bot_dumb.py`) so that it can load an external text file that contains frequently asked questions with the answers. The script will then provide the contents of the text file to the ChatGPTClient class inside the `chatgpt_client_for_qa_and_moderation.py` script who is responsible for creating the prompt and of course invoking the chat object of the OpenAI API for Python.

© Lydia Evelyn, Bruce Hopkins 2024
L. Evelyn and B. Hopkins, *Beginning ChatGPT for Python*, https://doi.org/10.1007/979-8-8688-0929-3_7

Making `tech_support_bot.py` More Intelligent

Listing 7-1 contains the full contents of the Frequently Asked Questions that the fictional customer support team has created based upon support tickets from users of the newly launched mobile banking application.

Listing 7-1. FAQ.txt

1. What is the Crooks Bank Mobile App?
The Crooks Bank Mobile App is a cutting-edge mobile banking app that allows you to manage your finances, make transactions, and access a wide range of banking services conveniently from your mobile device.

2. How can I download the Crooks Bank Mobile App?
You can download the Crooks Bank Mobile App from the App Store for iOS devices and Google Play for Android devices. Simply search for the "Crooks Bank Mobile App" and click the "Install" button.

3. Is the Crooks Bank Mobile App safe and secure?
Yes, the Crooks Bank Mobile App prioritizes your security. We use state-of-the-art encryption and security protocols to protect your data and transactions. Your information is safe with us.

4. What features does the Crooks Bank Mobile App offer?
The Crooks Bank Mobile App provides a variety of features, including:

- Account Management: View account balances, transaction history, and more.

- Transfer Funds: Easily transfer money between your accounts or to other bank accounts.

- Bill Payments: Pay bills and manage recurring payments.

- Deposit Checks: Snap photos of checks for remote deposit.

- ATM Locator: Find nearby ATMs and branches.

- Notifications: Receive alerts for account activity and important updates.

5. Can I link external accounts to the Crooks Bank Mobile App?
Yes, the Crooks Bank Mobile App supports linking external accounts from other financial institutions. You can monitor and manage your accounts from different banks in one place.

6. How can I reset my password if I forget it?
If you forget your password, simply click the "Forgot Password" option on the login screen. You'll receive instructions on how to reset your password.

7. What are the fees associated with the Crooks Bank Mobile App?
The Crooks Bank Mobile App aims to be transparent with its fees. You can find information on account fees, transaction charges, and other costs in the "Fees" section within the app or on our website.

8. Can I get customer support through the Crooks Bank Mobile App?
Absolutely! We offer customer support through our in-app messaging feature. You can also find our customer service contact information on our website.

9. Is the Crooks Bank Mobile App available for business accounts?
The Crooks Bank Mobile App primarily caters to personal banking needs. However, we have plans to introduce business banking services in the future.

10. How can I provide feedback or suggestions for the Crooks Bank Mobile App?
We welcome your feedback! You can submit suggestions and feedback through the "Contact Us" section in the app or on our website.

As you can see in the FAQ.txt file in Listing 7-1, there's no magic involved here. It's simply a list of questions and the answers. Now, let's see the newly modified tech_support_bot.py class. This is represented in Listing 7-2.

Listing 7-2. tech_support_smart_bot.py

```
"""

tech_support_bot.py

A Discord bot integrated with ChatGPT for automated responses in a
designated channel.
```

This script initializes a Discord bot using the discord.Client() class and listens for events such as messages being sent. When a message is received in the specified channel, the bot calls ChatGPT to generate a response based on the message content, and sends the response back to the same channel.

Requirements:
- discord (https://pypi.org/project/discord.py/)
- chatgpt_client (Assumed to be a custom module providing interaction with ChatGPT)

Usage:
1. Replace the DISCORD_TOKEN variable with your bot's token obtained from the Discord Developer Portal.
2. Adjust the CHANNEL_TO_WATCH variable to specify the name of the channel the bot should monitor and interact with.
3. Ensure that the chatgpt_client module is properly implemented and accessible.

Note: This script assumes the presence of a chatgpt_client module for interaction with the ChatGPT API.
"""

```
import discord
from chatgpt_client_for_qa_and_moderation import ChatGPTClient

# Bot's token for authentication
DISCORD_TOKEN = ''

# Name of the channel the bot should monitor and interact with
CHANNEL_TO_WATCH = 'q-and-a'

# Initialize the Discord client
discord_client = discord.Client()

# Create the system message for ChatGPT
system_message_to_chatgpt = "You are a virtual assistant that provides
support for the Crooks Bank banking app."

with open('FAQ.txt', 'r', encoding='utf-8') as file:
```

```python
    # Read the entire content of the file into a variable as a
      single string
    file_contents = file.read()

# Initialize the ChatGPT client
chatgpt_client_for_qa_and_moderation = ChatGPTClient(system_message_to_
chatgpt, file_contents)

# Event handler for when the bot is ready
@discord_client.event
async def on_ready():
    """

    Event handler triggered when the bot is successfully logged in and
    ready to receive events.
    """

    print('Logged in as', discord_client.user)
    print('------')

# Event handler for when a message is received
@discord_client.event
async def on_message(message):
    """

    Event handler triggered when a message is received.

    Parameters:
        message (discord.Message): The message received by the bot.

    Returns:
        None
    """

    # Ignore messages sent by the bot to prevent self-responses
    if message.author == discord_client.user:
        return

    # Ignore messages not in the specified "tech-support" channel
    if isinstance(message.channel, discord.TextChannel) and \
    message.channel.name != CHANNEL_TO_WATCH:
        return
```

```
async with message.channel.typing():
    # Call ChatGPT to generate a response based on the received message
    response_from_chatgpt = chatgpt_client_for_qa_and_moderation.send_
    message_from_discord(message.content)

# Construct a reply mentioning the message author and appending
  ChatGPT's response
reply = f'{message.author.mention} {response_from_chatgpt}'

# Send the reply to the same channel where the original message was
  received
await message.channel.send(reply)
```

```
# Run the bot with the provided token
discord_client.run(DISCORD_TOKEN)
```

Important Changes to Note from the Previous Version of the Tech Support Bot

Let's briefly analyze tech_support_smart_bot.py and discuss the changes that were made. The code snippet Listing 7-3 contains a portion of the full listing.

Listing 7-3. Setting the System Message and FAQ Info for tech_support_bot.py

```
# Create the system message for ChatGPT
system_message_to_chatgpt = "You are a Q and A bot for a discord group
dedicated to the banking app, Crook's Bank"

with open('FAQ.txt', 'r', encoding='utf-8') as file:
    # Read the entire content of the file into a variable as a
      single string
    file_contents = file.read()
```

As you can see, we're doing a few things at once.

First, as we have learned from the previous chapters in the book, you can dramatically set the tone of the conversation by providing a specific message to the system itself in your prompt. Therefore, we have a variable here containing the system message.

162

Next, we're defining another variable that provides a reference to the file path location where the frequently asked questions file is stored. Then we simply read the file – easy peasy.

Updates to the `on_message(message)` Function

When a message is received, be sure to notice the following lines:

```
@discord_client.event
async def on_message(message):
```

This function is the core part of our Discord bot. Whenever a message is posted in our Discord server, the function on_message() is called. The async keyword is important here because this enables on_message() to be called asynchronously, which is what we want, i.e., whenever a message is posted.

Note   A quick reminder about synchronous vs. asynchronous communication. A typical example of synchronous communication is like accessing a web server using a web browser. Once you send your request, you need to wait until you get a response. In order to view a different website, you need to send another request and wait again for the response.

A good example of asynchronous communication is emailing a friend or colleague. You can send 1, 2, 5, 10, or even 1000 emails to your friend, but they aren't necessarily *waiting* for your email. In other words, they aren't left in a "holding pattern" and stuck waiting for you to send something due to the way that email simply works. If and when an email arrives, your friend will get a notification.

Therefore, whenever a message is posted in our Discord server, the function on_message() is called with the message itself in the function parameters.

Now, let's further examine the following code from tech_support_bot.py:

```
async with message.channel.typing():
    # Call ChatGPT to generate a response based on the received message
    response_from_chatgpt = chatgpt_client_for_qa_and_moderation.send_
    message_from_discord(message.content)
```

```
# Construct a reply mentioning the message author and appending
  ChatGPT's response
reply = f'{message.author.mention} {response_from_chatgpt}'
```

Here, we provide a nice user experience and show the user that the bot is "typing," while the user's question is being sent to ChatGPT. When the response comes back, we provide the reply back to the user.

Analyzing chatgpt_client_for_qa_and_ moderation.py

Now, as we look further into Listing 7-2 above, tech_support_bot.py instantiates the ChatGPTClient object in the chatgpt_client_for_qa_and_moderation.py script which (as we stated previously) is very similar to the chatgpt_client.py script that we have used before. The complete source for chatgpt_client_for_qa_and_moderation.py is shown in Listing 7-4.

Listing 7-4. chatgpt_client_for_QA_and_moderation.py

```
import os
from dotenv import load_dotenv
from openai import OpenAI

class ChatGPTClient:
    def __init__(self, system_message, initial_instructions_to_chatgpt):
        # Load environment variables from .env
        load_dotenv()

        # Use the API key from the environment variable
        self.client = OpenAI()
        self.system_message = system_message
        self.initial_instructions_to_chatgpt = initial_instructions_
        to_chatgpt

    def send_message_from_discord(self, user_message):
        response = self.client.chat.completions.create(
            model="gpt-4",
            messages=[
```

```
            {
                "role": "system",
                "content": f'{self.system_message}'
            },
            {
                "role": "user",
                "content": f'{self.initial_instructions_to_chatgpt}'
            },
            {
                "role": "user",
                "content": f'{user_message}'
            }
        ],
        temperature=0.85,
        max_tokens=1921,
        top_p=1,
        frequency_penalty=0,
        presence_penalty=0
    )
    condensed_response = response.choices[0].message.content
    return condensed_response
```

Breaking Down the **ChatGPTClient** Class in Python So Our Bot Can Utilize ChatGPT

The Python class we've created, ChatGPTClient, serves as a crucial role in integrating the OpenAI API into our Discord bot. Let's take a look at the benefits:

The class is designed with modularity in mind, encapsulating all the functionalities for interacting with ChatGPT. In the __init__ method, we initialize the client passing in system message and contents of the FAQ.txt, as well as loading the OpenAI API key from the .env file.

Through the send_message_from_discord() method, the class makes communication with ChatGPT easier. Since the object is already constructed with the system message's initial instructions, the message from the Discord user is placed into the prompt as the user message, so that we can send the user's questions to ChatGPT programmatically.

The send_message_from_discord() method doesn't limit our use cases for this class. At the moment, we're using it for Q&A; however, any bot that uses this class would be able to prompt ChatGPT in any way for any purpose.

Finally, we're efficiently handling the response from the OpenAI API by extracting the content of the generated message and returning a condensed version. This allows our Discord bot to reply with just the information we're looking for, not the entire response that the Chat model returns. This is accomplished in a single line of code:

```
condensed_response = response.choices[0].message.content
```

Running Our Intelligent Q&A Bot: tech_support_bot.py

Now, let's run our new and improved Q&A Python Discord bot, tech_support_bot.py. After executing the app, be sure to return back to your Discord server and start asking questions. Figure 7-1 shows the bot in action.

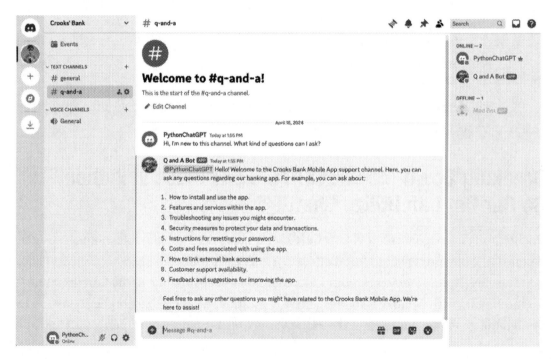

Figure 7-1. *Having a Discussion with Our Intelligent Discord Q&A Bot, tech_support_bot.py*

Listing 7-6 shows the conversation between us and the Discord bot.

Listing 7-5. Our First Conversation with the Intelligent Q&A Discord Bot

Me: Hi, I'm new to this channel. What kind of questions can I ask?

Q and A Bot: Hello! Welcome to the Crooks Bank Mobile App support channel. Here, you can ask any questions regarding our banking app. For example, you can ask about:
1. How to install and use the app.
2. Features and services within the app.
3. Troubleshooting any issues you might encounter.
4. Security measures to protect your data and transactions.
5. Instructions for resetting your password.
6. Costs and fees associated with using the app.
7. How to link external bank accounts.
8. Customer support availability.
9. Feedback and suggestions for improving the app.
Feel free to ask any other questions you might have related to the Crooks Bank Mobile App. We're here to assist!

Me: I have an old Blackberry phone, is the app supported on my device?

Q and A Bot: I'm sorry for the inconvenience, but at the moment, the Crooks Bank Mobile App is currently only available for iOS and Android devices. It is not supported on Blackberry or any other operating systems. You may still manage your bank accounts by accessing our website through your phone's browser.

Me: I'm an iPhone user. Can I sign into the app with face or touch ID?

Q and A Bot: Sure, here's how you can set up the Crooks Bank Mobile App on your iPhone:

1. Open the App Store on your iPhone.
2. In the search bar at the top, type in "Crooks Bank Mobile App" and tap "Search".
3. Once you can see the app in the search results, simply tap on the "Get" button to download it.

167

4. After the app downloads, tap "Open".

5. You'll have to agree to our Terms and Conditions upon the first launch.

6. If you're an existing Crooks Bank member, you can log in using your online banking user ID and password. If you're a new member, you'll need to register for an account.

7. Once you're logged in, you can set up Touch ID or Face ID for quicker, secure login in the future.

8. Now you can start using your Crooks Bank Mobile App to manage your finances, pay bills, make transactions, and more!

Please make sure you update the app regularly to access new features and improvements. If you have any challenges during setup, please reach out to us through the app's support feature or call our customer service.

We Have a Monumental Achievement…with One Slight Flaw

OK, if you step back and examine what we have achieved so far, you should realize that we're looking at what is nothing short of a monumental achievement. We have the following:

- A system made up of a few scripts that allows users to type in questions and get answers about how to use our mobile application.

- Using a simple text file, we can teach our bot how to answer the questions from our users. This text file can be edited by anyone in the company and can be used as a knowledge base to help improve the intelligence of the bot day by day. This is amazing stuff.

- Our system allows customers to type their questions using natural language, and the bot provides an intelligent answer back to them. And do you know what? Customers don't like reading FAQs – especially really long ones. However, using this system, they don't need to! All they have to do is ask the question that is relevant to them.

So, with all this that we have accomplished, there's one *gigantic* flaw that we can't ignore. In Listing 7-5 above, the bot said to the user:

```
Once you're logged in, you can set up Touch ID or Face ID for quicker,
secure login in the future.
```

No, no, no! Bad bot! In case you didn't read the Frequently Asked Questions file completely, please allow me to explain what went wrong here:

1. The `FAQ.txt` file in Listing 7-1 clearly states that the Crook's Bank mobile app is a mobile app. Currently, Touch ID can only be used on Apple desktop and laptop computers. So, this doesn't even make sense.

2. The `FAQ.txt` file has no mention of Face ID for authentication to the mobile app at all.

So unfortunately, ChatGPT is making up things that are simply not true and is assuming that certain features exist that are not present. So, for the purposes of true tech support, this is absolutely unacceptable.

So, how do we solve this problem? Think about how *you* could solve this problem for a second before reading the next section.

Update the System Message to ChatGPT, and Let's Try Again

Have you come up with a solution yet? One way to resolve this issue is to update the system message. Refer to the following line in Listing 7-2 above:

```
system_message_to_chatgpt = "You are a virtual assistant that provides
support for the Crooks Bank banking app. ";
```

Remember that the system message indicates to ChatGPT what its role is in the chat conversation. Right now, it is told to be a helpful assistant, and therefore, it has taken the liberty in order to guess that certain features exist within the mobile application. Now, let's ensure that ChatGPT does not provide any assumptions. Update the system message to be as shown below:

```
system_message_to_chatgpt = "You are a virtual assistant that provides
support for the Crooks Bank banking app. You will be provided Information
about the application, and users will ask you questions about the
application. Your role is to answer questions explicitly from the training
information. If you were not given an answer to a question, then provide
an apologetic message to the user explaining that you do not know the
answer.";
```

And that's it. The FAQ.txt file remains exactly the same as before, and all we needed to do is to update the system message to let ChatGPT know its role in the conversation. Listing 7-6 has the new conversation between us and the Discord bot.

Listing 7-6. Our Second (and Better) Conversation with the Intelligent Q&A Discord Bot

Me: How are you today?
Q and A Bot: As a virtual assistant, I don't have feelings or emotions, but I'm here and ready to assist you. How may I help you with the Crooks Bank Mobile App today?
Me: I have an old Blackberry phone, is the app supported on my device?
Q and A Bot: I'm sorry, but from the information provided, the Crooks Bank Mobile App can only be downloaded from the App Store for iOS devices and Google Play for Android devices. BlackBerry devices are not mentioned, therefore I cannot confirm that it would be compatible.
Me: So, if I use an iPhone, how do I setup the app?
Q and A Bot: To set up the Crooks Bank Mobile App on your iPhone, you can download it from the App Store. Simply search for "Crooks Bank Mobile App" and click the "Install" button. After the installation is finished, open the app and follow the prompts to set up your account. If you already have an account, use your login information to access your account through the app.

Now, that's a lot better! Our tech support bot is "sticking to the script" and is not allowed to make up or assume anything.

Conclusion

In this chapter, we've accomplished a lot! We have a fully functioning Discord bot that can be trained by anyone without any experience in AI, NLP, or machine learning using a simple text file. We learned that a "helpful assistant" may at times become *too helpful* and assume facts that are not true. However, we also reiterated the concept and the value of the system message, which is an important part of prompt engineering.

Now that we have made our Q&A Discord bot to be intelligent, let's find out how to make our content moderator bot to be intelligent as well!

CHAPTER 8

Adding Intelligence to Our Discord Bots, Part 2: Using Chat and Moderations Models for Content Moderation

In this chapter, we're going to take the steps necessary in order to make our content moderator discord bot artificially intelligent. Let's overview the changes that we're going to make:

- Create a new script for ourselves, `moderation_client.py`, to invoke the `OpenAI.moderations.create()` method of the OpenAI API. The Moderations model allows us to be aware when any textual content fits any of the following categories:

  - Hate

  - Hate/threatening

  - Harassment

  - Harassment/threatening

  - Self-harm

  - Self-harm/intent

  - Self-harm/instructions

© Lydia Evelyn, Bruce Hopkins 2024
L. Evelyn and B. Hopkins, *Beginning ChatGPT for Python*, https://doi.org/10.1007/979-8-8688-0929-3_8

- Sexual

- Sexual/minors

- Violence

- Violence/graphic

- Reuse our `chatgpt_client_for_qa_and_moderation.py` script from the previous chapter. In Chapter 7, it was used to invoke the OpenAI Chat class for Q&A purposes from our users. In this chapter, it will be used to invoke the Chat class again, but this time for moderation purposes. This is why the script is aptly named "`chatgpt_client_for_qa_and_moderation`" because it's used for Q&A in Chapter 7 but also for moderation in this chapter.

- Modify our `content_moderator_bot.py` script (formerly named, `content_moderator_bot_dumb.py`) so that it can invoke both the `moderation_client.py` and `chatgpt_client_for_qa_and_moderation.py`. If either script indicates that the content typed in the Discord channel is objectionable, then it will delete the message from that Discord channel. Remember, this bot watches all content in all channels of the Discord server!

Now, at this point, you may be asking yourself, if the Moderations class already knows how to flag any harmful content, then why do we need to use the Chat class as well? Good question.

Yes, the Moderations class will allow us to know about harmful content, but it **does not** inform us about any other types of unwanted content for our use case, such as when unscrupulous individuals try to lure our users into a scam. Remember, this is a Discord server for a banking app, so scammers would definitely love to target all the members of this Discord server since it's a central location full of bank users!

Therefore, we'll use the `moderation_client.py` to invoke the Moderations class to know if any content in the Discord server is harmful, and we'll reuse the `chatgpt_client_for_qa_and_moderation.py` from the last chapter in order to invoke the Chat method in order to be made aware of any other undesirable content is posted in the Discord server, such as scam attempts.

Using `OpenAI.moderations.create()` to Moderate Content

By using the Moderations models, developers are able to submit a string of text and to subsequently know if it's violent, hateful, and/or threatening or contains any form of harassment.

Table 8-1 describes the format of the parameters necessary to call the `OpenAI.moderations.create()` method. The service is very simple to use, since only one parameter is required to properly invoke the service.

Examining the Method Parameters

Table 8-1. *The Request Body for the Moderations Model*

Field	Type	Required?	Description
input	String or list	Required	The text that needs to be classified.
model	String Default: "omni-moderation-latest"	Optional	There are multiple content moderation models available for use, for example: • "omni-moderation-latest" • "text-moderation-stable" • "text-moderation-latest" By default, this is set to "omni-moderation-latest". It will be automatically upgraded over time, which ensures you're always using the most accurate model. If you decide to use any of the text based moderation models, then you are only able to submit text to be evaluated. The omni moderation models, however, are able to evaluate content as text and images. Therefore choose the model that works best for your use case.

175

Handling the Response

After successfully invoking the Moderations model, the method will provide a response
with the structure shown in Table 8-2.

Moderation (Dictionary)

Table 8-2. *The Structure of the Moderation Response*

Field	Type	Description
id	String	A unique identifier for the moderation request.
model	String	The model used to perform the moderation request.
results	List	A list of moderation objects.
↳ flagged	Boolean	Flags if the content violates OpenAI's usage policies.
↳ categories	List	A list of the categories and whether they're being flagged or not.
↳↳ hate	Boolean	This indicates whether or not the text given expresses, incites, or promotes hate based on race, gender, religion, ethnicity, nationality, disability status, sexual orientation, or caste.
↳↳ hate/threatening	Boolean	This indicates whether or not the text given contains hateful content that also threatens violence or serious harm toward the targeted group based on biases expressed above.
↳↳ harassment	Boolean	This indicates whether or not the text given contains content that expresses, incites, or promotes harassing language toward any target.
↳↳ harassment/ threatening	Boolean	This indicates whether or not the text given contains harassment content that also threatens violence or serious harm toward any target.
↳↳ self-harm	Boolean	This indicates whether or not the text given contains content that promotes, encourages, or depicts acts of self-harm, for example, suicide, cutting, and eating disorders.

(continued)

Table 8-2. (*continued*)

Field	Type	Description
↳↳ self-harm/intent	Boolean	This indicates whether or not the text given contains content in which the speaker expresses that they are engaging or intend to engage in acts of self-harm, such as suicide, cutting, and eating disorders.
↳↳ self-harm/instructions	Boolean	This indicates whether or not the text given contains content that encourages the performing acts of self-harm, such as suicide, cutting, and eating disorders. This includes content that gives instructions or advice on how to commit such acts.
↳↳ sexual	Boolean	This indicates whether or not the text given contains content meant to arouse sexual excitement, such as the description of sexual activity. This includes content that promotes sexual services; however, this **excludes** topics such as sex education and wellness.
↳↳ sexual/minors	Boolean	This indicates whether or not the text given contains content that includes an individual under the age of 18.
↳↳ violence	Boolean	This indicates whether or not the text given contains content depicting death, violence, or physical injury.
↳↳ violence/graphic	Boolean	This indicates whether or not the text given contains content depicting death, violence, or physical injury in graphic detail.
↳ category_scores	List	A list of the categories along with the scores given by the model.
↳↳ hate	Number	Score for the category "hate."
↳↳ hate/threatening	Number	Score for the category "hate/threatening."
↳↳ harassment	Number	Score for the category "harassment."
↳↳ harassment/ threatening	Number	Score for the category "harassment/threatening."
↳↳ self-harm	Number	Score for the category "self-harm."

(*continued*)

Table 8-2. (*continued*)

Field	Type	Description
↳↳ self-harm/intent	Number	Score for the category "self-harm/intent."
↳↳ self-harm/instructions	Number	Score for the category "self-harm/instructions."
↳↳ sexual	Number	Score for the category "sexual."
↳↳ violence	Number	Score for the category "violence."
↳↳ violence/graphic	Number	Score for the category "violence/graphic."

The listing below is an example of the Moderation response after invoking the
Moderations model. Table 8-2 looks a little complex, but as you can see, if any of the
categories are labeled as "true," then the **results.flagged** node is labeled as "true."

Take a look at Listing 8-1 for a practical example of the Moderation response.

Listing 8-1. The Moderation Response

```
{
  "id": "modr-XXXXX",
  "model": "text-moderation-005",
  "results": [
    {
      "flagged": true,
      "categories": {
        "sexual": false,
        "hate": false,
        "harassment": false,
        "self-harm": false,
        "sexual/minors": false,
        "hate/threatening": false,
        "violence/graphic": false,
        "self-harm/intent": false,
        "self-harm/instructions": false,
```

```
      "harassment/threatening": true,
      "violence": true,
    },
    "category_scores": {
      "sexual": 1.2282071e-06,
      "hate": 0.010696256,
      "harassment": 0.29842457,
      "self-harm": 1.5236925e-08,
      "sexual/minors": 5.7246268e-08,
      "hate/threatening": 0.0060676364,
      "violence/graphic": 4.435014e-06,
      "self-harm/intent": 8.098441e-10,
      "self-harm/instructions": 2.8498655e-11,
      "harassment/threatening": 0.63055265,
      "violence": 0.99011886,
    }
  }
 ]
}
```

Creating Our Client for the Moderations Model: `moderation_client.py`

Listing 8-2 is our client to invoke the Moderations model. Take a look at it, and then we'll discuss the important parts afterward.

Listing 8-2. moderation_client.py

```python
import os
from dotenv import load_dotenv
from openai import OpenAI

class ModerationResponse:
    def __init__(self):
        load_dotenv()
        self.client = OpenAI()
```

```
def moderate_text(self, text):
    moderation = self.client.moderations.create(input=text)
    return moderation
```

In the previous chapters in this book, we created client scripts for the
various methods of the classes of the OpenAI API. Therefore, the class above,
ModerationResponse in `moderation_client.py`, should look quite familiar. At the end
of the day, we have a simple function, `moderate_text()`, which allows us to pass the text
that we want to evaluate and returns the response.

Making content_moderator_bot.py More Intelligent

Now that we have `moderation_client.py` to invoke the Moderations model, let's take a
look at the updated `content_moderator_bot.py` (formerly named, `content_moderator_
bot_dumb.py`) that will use the `moderation_client.py` to check for harmful content
and the `chatgpt_client_for_qa_and_moderation.py` (unmodified from the previous
chapter) to check for potential scams.

Listing 8-3 is the full source code for our intelligent Discord moderator bot,
`content_moderator_bot.py`.

Listing 8-3. content_moderator_bot.py

```
"""

content_moderation_bot.py

A Discord bot integrated with ChatGPT and a moderation service for
automated content moderation in Discord servers.

This script initializes a Discord bot using the discord.Client() class and
listens for events such as messages being sent. When a message is received,
it calls both the ChatGPT API and a moderation service to analyze the
message content for rule violations. If the message is flagged by either
service, it deletes the message and sends a notification to the user
explaining why it was deemed inappropriate.
```

Requirements:
- discord (https://pypi.org/project/discord.py/)
- chatgpt_client_for_qa_and_moderation (Assumed to be a custom module providing interaction with ChatGPT)
- moderation_client (Assumed to be a custom module providing interaction with a moderation service)

Usage:
1. Replace the DISCORD_TOKEN variable with your bot's token obtained from the Discord Developer Portal.
2. Ensure that the chatgpt_client_for_qa_and_moderation and moderation_client modules are properly implemented and accessible.

Note: This script assumes the presence of modules for interaction with ChatGPT and a moderation service.
"""

```
import discord
from chatgpt_client_for_qa_and_moderation import ChatGPTClient
from moderation_client import ModerationResponse

# Bot's token for authentication
DISCORD_TOKEN = ''

# Initialize the Discord client
discord_client = discord.Client()

# Create the system message for ChatGPT
system_message_to_chatgpt = """
        You are the automated moderator assistant for a Discord server.
        Review each message for the following rule violations:
        1. Sensitive information
        2. Abuse
        3. Inappropriate comments
        4. Spam, for example; a message in all capital letters, the same
           phrase or word being repeated over and over, more than 3
           exclamation marks or question marks.
        5. Advertisement
```

6. External links

7. Political messages or debate

8. Religious messages or debate

If any of these violations are detected, respond with "FLAG" (in uppercase without quotation marks). If the message adheres to the rules, respond with "SAFE" (in uppercase without quotation marks).
    """

```python
initial_instructions_to_chatgpt = "Analyze the following message for rule violations:"

# Initialize the ChatGPT client
chatgpt_client_for_qa_and_moderation = ChatGPTClient(system_message_to_
chatgpt, initial_instructions_to_chatgpt)

# Initialize the Moderation client
moderation_client = ModerationResponse()

# Event handler for when the bot is ready
@discord_client.event
async def on_ready():

    """

    Event handler triggered when the bot is successfully logged in and
    ready to receive events.
    """

    print('Logged in as', discord_client.user)
    print('------')

# Event handler for when a message is received
@discord_client.event
async def on_message(message):

    """

    Event handler triggered when a message is received.

    Parameters:
        message (discord.Message): The message received by the bot.
```

```python
    Returns:
        None
    """

    # Ignore messages sent by the bot to prevent self-responses
    if message.author == discord_client.user:
        return

    # Call the Moderation method to check for harmful content
    moderation_response = moderation_client.moderate_text(message.content)

    # Call ChatGPT to generate a response based on the received message
    response_from_chatgpt = chatgpt_client_for_qa_and_moderation.send_
    message_from_discord(message.content)

    # Check for if the message from ChatGPT is "FLAG" or if the moderation
    response indicates that the input has been flagged
    if response_from_chatgpt == "FLAG" or moderation_response.results[0].
    flagged:

    # Delete the message
        await message.delete()

        # Mention the user who sent the inappropriate message
        author_mention = message.author.mention

        # Send a message mentioning the user and explaining why it was
        inappropriate
        await message.channel.send(f"{author_mention} This comment was
        deemed inappropriate for this channel. " +
        "If you believe this to be in error, please contact one of the
         human server moderators.")

# Run the bot with the provided token
discord_client.run(DISCORD_TOKEN)
```

Updates to the on_message(message) Function

After a message is received in any channel of the Discord server, the
on_message(message) function is invoked asynchronously. Here's the most important
change to be aware of:

```
# Call the Moderation model to check for harmful content
moderation_response = moderation_client.moderate_text(message.content)
```

```
# Call ChatGPT to generate a response based on the received message
response_from_chatgpt = chatgpt_client_for_qa_and_moderation.send_
message_from_discord(message.content)
```

```
# Check for if the message from ChatGPT is "FLAG" or if the moderation
response indicates that the input has been flagged
if response_from_chatgpt == "FLAG" or moderation_response.results[0].
flagged:
```

```
# Delete the message
    await message.delete()

    # Mention the user who sent the inappropriate message
    author_mention = message.author.mention

    # Send a message mentioning the user and explaining why it was
    inappropriate
    await message.channel.send(f"{author_mention} This comment was
    deemed inappropriate for this channel. " +
    "If you believe this to be in error, please contact one of the
    human server moderators.")
```

Here, we take each message that was posted in the Discord server and check it with
both the Moderations class and the Chat method. If either method return to inform us
that the message is flagged, then we delete the message in the channel and inform the
user that their message violated the rules.

Now that our content moderator Discord bot is intelligent, let's give it a try!

Running Our Intelligent Content Moderator Bot: content_moderator_bot.py

Now let's run our new and improved content moderator Python Discord bot, content_moderator_bot.py. After executing the app, be sure to return back to your Discord server and start asking questions. Figure 8-1 shows the bot in action.

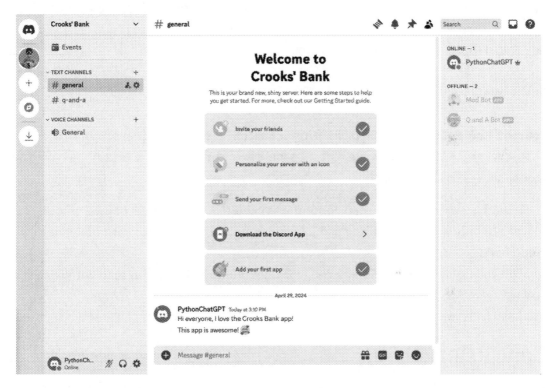

Figure 8-1. *Having a Discussion with Our Intelligent Discord Content Moderator Bot: content_moderator_bot.py*

Listing 8-4 shows a conversation between us and the Discord bot in order to test and see what it can do.

Listing 8-4. Our Offensive Conversation with the Intelligent Moderator Discord Bot

Me: Hi everyone, I love the Crooks Bank app!

Me: This app is awesome! 🥴

Me: Come to my website! http://www.google.com

Content Mod Bot: @PythonChatGPT This comment was deemed inappropriate for this channel. If you believe this to be in error, please contact one of the human server moderators.

Me: I'm sorry for breaking the rules. I'm a different person now

Me: But I have some sad news for you

Me: I want to ⋯ everyone

Content Mod Bot: @PythonChatGPT This comment was deemed inappropriate for this channel. If you believe this to be in error, please contact one of the human server moderators.

In both cases when unwanted content was posted in any channel of the Discord server, not only was the offending user called out but the bad message was deleted. Good bot!

Did you notice that the Moderation and Chat methods are able to read emojis as well?

Conclusion

In this chapter, we created a fully functioning content moderator for our entire Discord server! We leveraged both the Moderations and Chat methods from OpenAI to create a custom content moderator that not only flags unsafe content like hateful and threatening messages but also prevents the users of the Discord server from being subject to unwanted solicitations.

Exercises Left for the Reader

Although we accomplished a lot in this chapter (as well as in this book!), there's still one more thing that we can do to improve the code. For example:

- The individual Discord bots that we created are aware to not respond
  to messages that they send themselves. However, the bots are not
  yet aware that they shouldn't respond to messages sent by **other
  bots**. In other words, if you run both bots at the same time, and
  someone posts something bad in the "q-and-a" channel, the content
  moderator will, of course, delete the message and inform everyone
  that the message was deleted. However, since the tech support bot
  doesn't know that it shouldn't respond to other bots, it will try to
  create a response. Of course, bots should not talk to other bots.

APPENDIX 1

List of OpenAI Models

After executing the code in Listing 2-4, model_lister.py, you will be presented with a response object that has a list of the OpenAI models available to you. The table below shows a snapshot of the response.

ID	Object	Created	Owned By
gpt-4-turbo	model	1712361441	system
gpt-4-turbo-2024-04-09	model	1712601677	system
tts-1	model	1681940951	openai-internal
tts-1-1106	model	1699053241	system
chatgpt-4o-latest	model	1723515131	system
dall-e-2	model	1698798177	system
whisper-1	model	1677532384	openai-internal
gpt-3.5-turbo-instruct	model	1692901427	system
gpt-3.5-turbo	model	1677610602	openai
gpt-3.5-turbo-0125	model	1706048358	system
babbage-002	model	1692634615	system
davinci-002	model	1692634301	system
gpt-4o-mini-2024-07-18	model	1721172717	system
gpt-4o	model	1715367049	system
dall-e-3	model	1698785189	system
gpt-4o-mini	model	1721172741	system
gpt-4o-2024-08-06	model	1722814719	system

(*continued*)

© Lydia Evelyn, Bruce Hopkins 2024
L. Evelyn and B. Hopkins, *Beginning ChatGPT for Python*, https://doi.org/10.1007/979-8-8688-0929-3

ID	Object	Created	Owned By
gpt-4o-2024-05-13	model	1715368132	system
o1-preview	model	1725648897	system
gpt-4o-audio-preview-2024-10-01	model	1727389042	system
o1-mini-2024-09-12	model	1725648979	system
gpt-4o-audio-preview	model	1727460443	system
tts-1-hd	model	1699046015	system
tts-1-hd-1106	model	1699053533	system
o1-preview-2024-09-12	model	1725648865	system
o1-mini	model	1725649008	system
gpt-4-1106-preview	model	1698957206	system
text-embedding-ada-002	model	1671217299	openai-internal
gpt-3.5-turbo-16k	model	1683758102	openai-internal
text-embedding-3-small	model	1705948997	system
text-embedding-3-large	model	1705953180	system
gpt-4o-realtime-preview-2024-10-01	model	1727131766	system
gpt-4o-realtime-preview	model	1727659998	system
gpt-3.5-turbo-1106	model	1698959748	system
gpt-4-0613	model	1686588896	openai
gpt-4-turbo-preview	model	1706037777	system
gpt-4-0125-preview	model	1706037612	system
gpt-4	model	1687882411	openai
gpt-3.5-turbo-instruct-0914	model	1694122472	system

Index

Printed in the United States
by Baker & Taylor Publisher Services